The Birds of Haiti and San Domin Cory

Publisher's Note

The book descriptions we ask booksellers to display prominently warn that this is an historic book with numerous typos or missing text; it is not indexed or illustrated.

The book was created using optical character recognition software. The software is 99 percent accurate if the book is in good condition. However, we do understand that even one percent can be an annoying number of typos! And sometimes all or part of a page may be missing from our copy of the book. Or the paper may be so discolored from age that it is difficult to read. We apologize and gratefully acknowledge Google's assistance.

After we re-typeset and design a book, the page numbers change so the old index and table of contents no longer work. Therefore, we often remove them.

Our books sell so few copies that you would have to pay hundreds of dollars to cover the cost of our proof reading and fixing the typos, missing text and index. Instead we usually let our customers download a free copy of the original typo-free scanned book. Simply enter the barcode number from the back cover of the paperback in the Free Book form at www.general-books.net. You may also qualify for a free trial membership in our book club to download up to four books for free. Simply enter the barcode number from the back cover onto the membership form on our home page. The book club entitles you to select from more than a million books at no additional charge. Simply enter the title or subject onto the search form to find the books.

If you have any questions, could you please be so kind as to consult our Frequently Asked Questions page at www.general-books.net/faqs.cfm? You are also welcome to contact us there.

General Books LLC™, Memphis, USA, 2012.

CHARLES B. CORY,
Fellow Of The Linnean Society Of London; Fellow Of The Zoological Society Of London; Member Of The American Ornithologists' Union; Of The British Ornithologists' Union; Of The Societe Zoologique Ok France; Of The Society D'acclimatation Of France, Etc.; Corr. Memb. Of The New York Academy Of Sciences, Etc., Etc.; Author Of "the Beautiful And Curious Birds Of The World," "The Birds Of The Bahama Islands," Etc.

ESTES & LAURIAT, BOSTON, U. S. A. 1885. *L.*

TABLE OF CONTENTS.
PAGE
INDEX TO PLATES. 13
INTRODUCTION 15
TURDID 17
TURDUS 17
MIMOCICHLA. 18
MIMUS 21
SYLVICOLIDE. 23
MINOTILTA 23
PARULA 24
DENDRCECA 25
SEIURUS 34
GEOTHLYPIS 36
MICROLIGEA 38
SETOPHAGA 40
CCEREBIDE 41
CERTHIOLA 41
HIRUNDINIDE 44
PROGNE 44
HIRUNDO 45
PETROCHELIDON 47
VIREONID 49
VIREO 49
PAGE
CYPSELIDE............. 87
CYPSELUS............. 87
NEPHCECETES........... 88
TROCHILID:............ 9

LAMPORNIS............. 9
MELLISUGA............. 92
SPORADINUS............ 93
TROGONIDE............. 95
TEMNOTROGON............ 95
CUCULIDE............. 98
SAUROTHERA............ 98
CROTOPHAGA............100
COCCYGUS............. 101
CEDINI
CERYLE............. 103
TODIDE............. 15
TODUS............. 105
PICIDE............. 19
HCUMNUS............. 109
CENTURUS............. 1n
PSITTACIDE............. "3
CONURUS............. 113
CHRYSOTIS............. 115
STRIGIDE........... "7
STRIX............. 117
SPEOTYTO. 118
r
PROCELLARIDE.
PUFFINUS.
PODICIPID.E.
PODICEPS.
INDEX
189-198
INDEX OF PLATES.
MIMOCICHLA ARDESIACA.
MIMOCICHLA ARDESIACA (
MICROLIGEA PALUSTRIS.
HIRUNDO SCLATERI
MYIADESTES MONTANUS
SPINDALIS MULTICOLOR.
PHOENICOPHILUS D
CALYPTOPHILUS FF
EUPHOMA MUSICA
LOXIMITRIS DOMINICENSIS
ICTERUS DOMINICENSIS.
TEMNOTROGON ROSEIG
PICUMNUS LAWRENCEI
CONURUS CHLOPTERUS
ACCII'ITER FRINGILLOIDES
RUPORNIS RIDGWAYI.
RUPORNIS RIDGWAYI (
CEDICNEMUS DOMINIC!
PARRA GYMNOSTOMA.
HEADS.

Plate 21.
CERTHIOLA BANANIVORA PETROCHELIDON FULVA PROGNE UOMINICENSIS DULUS DOMINICUS 201 LOXIGILLA VIOLACEA PHCENICOPHILUS PALMARUM PHONIPARA ZENA PHONIPARA OLIVACEA

Plate 22.
QUISCALUS NIGER PITANGUS GABBII MYIARCHUS DOMINICENSIS CONTOPUS HISPANIOLENSIS EMPIDONAX NANUS 203 LAMPORNIS DOMINICUS 3 2 SPORADINUS ELEGANS $ y MELLISUGA MINIMA NEPHCECETES NIGER CYPSELUS PHCENICOBIUS

Plate 23.
TODUS SUBULATUS TODUS ANGUSTIROSTRIS CENTURUS STRIATUS S 9 205 SAUROTHERA DOMINICENSIS CHRYSOTIS SALLJEI. INTRODUCTION.

The island of Santo Domingo, or San Domingo, as it is often called, is situated in north latitude 18 20', and longitude 68 40' west from Greenwich.

The avi fauna of the island is especially interesting to ornithologists on account of the many genera and species which are restricted to it. Thirty-two species are peculiar to San Domingo, which are as follows: —

MlMUS DOMINICUS.
Microligea Palustris.
Certhiola Bananivora.
HlRUNDO SCLATERI.
Dulus Dominicus.
Myiadestes Montanus.
Spendalis Multicolor.
Plkknicophilus Palmarum.
Phcenicophilus Dominicensis.
Calyptophilus Frugivorus.
Euphonia Musica.
Loxiiiitris Dominicensis.
Icterus Dominicensis.
Quiscalus Niger.
Corvus Solitarius.
PlTANGUS GABBII.
Myiarchus Dominicensis.
Contopus Hispaniolensis.
Empidonax Nanus.
Lampornis Dominicus.
Sporadinus Elegans.
Temnotrogon Roseigaster.
Saurothera Dominicensis.
Todus Subulatus.
Todus Angustirostris.
Picumnus Lawrencei.
Centurus Striatus.
Conurus Chloropterus.
Chrysotis Sall.ei.
Strix Glaucops.
Rupornis Ridgwayi.
Cedicnemus Dominicensis.

Guinea Hens *(Numida meleagris)* are common in some localities, having been introduced many years ago; and it is claimed by the inhabitants that Peacocks are found in some of the mountains in the southeastern part of the island.

Several of the forms which occur in San Domingo vary slightly in coloration and marking from specimens taken in other localities, and might perhaps represent local races. This is especially shown in *Spcotyto, Corvus, Ortyx,* and several others; but I have deemed it advisable to err in being rather too conservative than otherwise.

The generic name *Ligca* being preoccupied in zoology, I have substituted for it the name *Mieroligea* (Auk, I. p. 290, 1884). The single known species will therefore stand as *Mieroligea palusfris,* instead of *Ligea palustris,* as on page 38 of this work.

C. B. CORY.
Genus: TURDUS. Linn.
TURDUS: LINiV., SYST. NAT., I. p. 291 (1766).
TURDUS ALICIA. *Baird. Turdus alicia.* Baird, Cass. and Lawr., Bds. N. Amer. , p. 217, pi. 81 (1858). — Sclater, P. Z. S., 1859, p. 326.— Baird, Review, I. p. 21 (1864). — Bd., Bwr. and Ridgw. , Hist. N. A. Bds., I. p. 11 (1874).— Tacz., Bull. Soc. Zool. France, 1876, p. 148.— Salv. and Godm., Biol. Centr. Amer. Zool. Aves, I. p. 12 (1879). — Seebohm, Cat. Bds. Brit. Mus., V. p. 202. *Turdus swainsoni var. alicia.* Coues, Key N. A. Bds., p. 73 (1872). *Turdus swainsoni b. alicia.* Coues, Bds. Colorado Vail., p. 35 (1878). *Sp. Char.* — Above, dull olive; sides of the head, ash gray; underparts, including chin and throat, white, the latter showing a faint tawny tinge; the breast and sides of the throat showing arrowshaped markings of plumbeous brown; sides of the body and axillaries, olivaceous gray; legs and bill, brownish.

The sexes are similar.

Length 6.60; wing 3.75; tail 2.70; tarsus 1.1o; bill.50.

This species is a winter visitant, and not at all common. Three specimens were procured in the vicinity of Puerto Plata during December and January. Their measurements are as follows: — *Sp. Char., Male.* — General plumage plumbeous, a patch of black extending from below, and in front of the eye, to the base of the upper mandable; throat, white, streaked heavily with black; top of head somewhat dotted with brown; underparts, pale plumbeous, becoming white on the abdomen and crissum; primaries, dark brown, the outer webs edged with plumbeous gray; same marking, but much broader edging on the secondaries; tail, dark brown, the outer feathers broadly tipped with white, the white becoming less and less to the fourth, which is only narrowly touched; but the tail marking varies in different specimens and seasons; bill, eyelids, and legs, vermilionorange; iris, reddish brown.

Length 10; wing 5.20; tail 4.70; tarsus 1.40; bill.75.

The sexes are similar.

The present Thrush is found wherever there are large trees in all parts of the island. It was very abundant in the vicinity of Fort Jacques, at an altitude of 2,500 feet above the sea level. On the coast it prefers the thickest and most secluded localities; but high up in the mountains we often observed it flying about in the open. Its note somewhat resembles that of the Robin *(Turdus migratorius).* The breeding season is in December and January. A nest taken near Puerto Plata, Jan. 9, contained two eggs, in which incubation had already commenced. The nest was built about three feet from the ground, in the crotch of a small tree, surrounded by a dense growth of underbrush. The eggs are dull bluish white, heavily blotched with brown, and measure!rWxTVr-The food consists mainly of insects and berries.

Subfamily, MIMIN/E.
Genus: MIMUS. Boie.
MIMUS: BOIE., ISIS, p. 972, 1826.

MIMUS DOMINICUS. *(Linn.) Turdus dominicus.* Linn., Syst. Nat., I. p. 295 (1766). *Turdus merle.* Miil!., S. N. Anhang., p. 139 (1766). — Cass., Proc. Phil. Acad., p. 249 (1864). *Mitnus dominicus.* Gray, Gen. Bds., I. p. 221 (1847).— " Bp., Consp.,

I. p. 276 (1853)." —Salle (Sclater), P. Z. S., 1857, p. 232.—

Sclater, P. Z. S., 1859, p. 341. — Sharpe, Cat. Bds. Brit. Mus., VI. p. 341 (1881). *Mimus polyglottus var, dominicus.* Bryant, Proc. Boston Soc. Nat.

Hist., XI. p. 93 (1866). *Mimus orphcus dominicus.* Cory, Bull. Nutt. Orn. Club, VI. p. 151 (1881).

Sp. Char., Male. — Above, grayish brown, showing ashy on the back; underparts, white, slightly tinged with ashy on the breast; wings, brown; all of the primaries heavily marked with, and the eighth and ninth almost entirely, white; tail, dark brown, having the first two and inner web of third feathers white; bill, black; legs, brownish. Sexes are similar.

Length 8.50; wing 4; tail 4.10; tarsus 1.20; bill.64.

The present species is very closely allied to *M. orpheus;* some specimens from San Domingo are apparently the same as typical *M. orpheus* from Jamaica; but several specimens in the series before me vary sufficiently to characterize at least a geographical race; and although allowing it to retain its rank as a species, I am inclined to believe that its true position is that of a variety of *M. orpheus.*

This mocking-bird is abundant on the west coast of the island. We found it common among the mountains in the neighborhood of Le Coup. No specimens were observed in San Domingo, although it without doubt ranges over the whole island.

The following measurements are from specimens now before me:
No. Date. Sex. Mus. Locality. Length. Wing. Tail. Tarsus.
1130 Feb. 23, 1881. $ C.B.C. j LeH2"P' 8.5 4. 4.10 1.20 *Margarops fuscatus (Vicill).* Veillot, in Ois. de i'Am., Sept., II. p. 1, pi. 57, bis, gives this bird as being found in San Domingo. I know of no instance of its capture, although it may possibly occur, as it is common on the island of Inagua. FAMILY SYLVICOLID/E.

Subfamily, S Y L VICO LIN/E.
Genus: MNIOTILTA. Vieill.
MNIOTILTA: VIEILLOT, ANALYSE, 45, 1816.
MNIOTILTA VARIA. *(Linn.) Motacilla varia.* Linn., Syst. Nat., I. (1766). *Certhia varia.* Vieill., Ois. Am., Sept., II. p. 69, 1807; and Orn.

Biog., I. p. 452 (1832).
Mniotilta varia. Vieill., "Anal. (1816), and Gal. Ois., I., 1834." —

Aud., Bds. Amer. Zool. Aves, II. p. 105(1841). — Bd., Bwr. and Ridgw., Hist. N. A. Bds., I. p. 180 (1874). —Cones, Bds. N. W., p. 45 (1874). — Cory, Bds. Bahama I., p. 54 (1880). — Cory, Bull. Nutt. Orn. Club, VI. p. 151 (1881).

Sylvla varia. Bp. Synopsis, p. 81 (1828). *Sylvicola varia.* "Rich. List (1837)." *Certhia maculata.* Wils., Am. Orn., III. p. 22 (1811). *Mniotilta borealis.* "Nutt. Man, 2 Ed., I. p. 704 (1840). " *Winter Plumage, Male.* — Upper parts, black, the feathers broadly edged with brownish white; a superciliary line of brownish white; underparts, white, with faint ash-colored stripes-upon the sides of the breast, shading into brownish upon the sides of the belly and crissum; two clearly defined bands upon the wings; tail, black, edged with whitish; inner webs of the two outer tail-feathers tipped with white. *Female.* — Similar to the male, having the underparts white, faintly marked with blackish on the sides.

Length 5.05; wing 2.75; tail 2.10; tarsus.80; bill.50.

A not uncommon winter visitant, generally found near the coast.
Genus: PARULA. Bonap.
PARULA: BOXAPARTE, GF.OG. AND COMT. LIST, 1838.'
PARULA AMERICANA. *(Linn.) Parus americanus.* Linn., Syst. Nat., I. p 190 (1758).
Motocilla americana. Gm., Syst. Nat., I. p. 960(1788).
Sylvia americana. Lath., Ind. Orn., II. p. 520 (1790).
Sylvicola americana. Aud., Bds. Am., II. p. 57 (1841), pi. 91.
Parula americana. Gosse, Bds. Jam., p. 154(1847). — Bd., Bwr. and Ridgw., Hist. N. A. Bds., I. p. 208 (1874).—Coues, Bds. N. W., p. 46 (1874). — Godman and Salvin, Biol. Cent. Amer. Zool.

Aves, Pt. VI. p. 119 (1sSo). — Cory, Bds. Bahama I., p. 55 (1880).

— Cory, Bull. Nutt. Orn. Club, VI. p. 151 (1881). *Campsothlypis americana.* "Cab., Mus. Hein., 1850, 20." *Sylvia torquata.* Vieill., Ois. Am., Sept., II. p. 38 (1807). *Sylvia pusilla.* Wils., Am. Orn., IV. p. 17 (1811).

Winter Plumage, Male.— Above, blue; a slight tinge of yellow upon the crown and nape; middle of the back with a broad patch of greenish yellow; throat and breast, yellow, with an imperfect band of blue across the jugulum, anterior to one of brown intermixed with yellow; a small white spot on the eyelid; sides of the head, ashy blue; two well-defined white bands on the wings; belly, white, shading into ash upon the side and flanks, and yellowish upon the crissum; tail, with the exception of the two middle feathers, showing a patch of white upon the inner webs. *Winter Plumage, Female.* — Above, olive; underparts, dull white, sometimes showing a tinge of brownish on the breast. Length 4.40; wing 2.35; tail 2; tarsus. 65.

The present species is a common winter visitant.

Winter Plumage, Male.— Upper parts, olive green, slightly marked with black; feathers of the head, black, edged with gray, giving the top of the head a mottled appearance; ear coverts showing a very slight tinge of chestnut; superciliary stripe, yellow; a yellow band passing round the sides of the throat, nearly joining above; underparts, bright yellow, streaked with black; quills and tail, dark brown, edged with yellowish white; three outer tail-feathers with patch of white upon the inner webs; rump, yellow; crissum, yellowish white. *Winter Plumage, Female.*— Above, olivaceous ash, showing yellowish on the rump; no black or chestnut about the head; tail spots not so clear as in the

male; beneath, whitish, slightly tinged with yellow on the breast, and streaked with dusky, not black, as in the male.
Length 4.75; wing 2.80; tail 2; tarsus. 80; bill.40.

A winter visitor; very abundant in February and March.

Sylvia pusilla. Wils., Am. Orn., V. p. 100 (1812). *Sylvicola canadensis.* "Sv. and Rich., Rep. Brit. Assoc., 1837," and Bds. Am., II. p. 63 (1841).

Sylvicola pannosa. Gosse, Bds. Jamaica, p. 162 (1847).

Adult, Male. — Above, slaty blue; sides of the head, throat, and sides of the body, black; rest of underparts, white; a band of white on the primaries; tail, dark brown, blotched with white. *Adult, Female.* — Smaller than the male; above, olive green, reaching the sides of the throat; underparts, pale greenish yellow.
Length 5; wing 2 40; tail.90; tarsus.72; bill.36.

The present species is a winter visitant; abundant in February and March.

Sylvia pcnsilis. "Lath., Ind. Orn., II. p. 520 (1790)." — Aud., Orn. Biog., I. p. 434 (1831). *Sylvicola pcnsilis.* Aud., Ikls., II. p. 32 (1841). — Gosse, Bds. Jam., p. 156 (1847). *Rhimanphus pcnsilis.* "Cab., J. f. O., III. p. 474 (1855)." *Winter Plumage, Male.—* Above, grayish blue; forehead, lores, cheeks and sides of the throat, and streaks on the sides of the breast, black; superciliary line, white, with a yellowish tinge at the base of the bill; small white line under the eye; sides of the neck behind the cheek-patch, and two bands on the wings, white; throat and part of breast, bright yellow; lower part of breast and belly, white, the latter with broad black stripes upon the sides; the outer webs of the three outer tail-feathers patched with white.

Female. — Slightly smaller and paler, showing a trace of brown upon the belly.
Length 5.15; wing 2.60; tail 2.20; tarsus.65; bill.50.

This species is a common winter visitant.

DENDRCECA MACULOSA. *(Cm.) Motacilla maculosa.* Gm.. Syst. Nat., I. p. 984 (1788). *Sylvia maculosa.* Lath. , Ind. Orn., II. p. 536 (1790). — Aud., Orn. Biog., I. p. 260 (1831). *Sylvicola maculosa.* Sv. and Rich., Faun. B. Am., II. p. 213 (1831). — Aud., Bds. Am., II. p. 65 (1841). *Dcudrceca maculosa.* Bd. , B. N. A., p. 284 (1858); Rev., p. 206 (1865). —Gund., J. f. O., p. 326 (1861). — Coues, Bds. N. W., p. 63 (1874).— Bd., Bwr. and Ridgw., Hist. N. A. Bds., I. p. 232 (1874). — Godman and Salvin, Biol. Centr. Amer. Zool. Aves, Pt. IX. p. 129 (1881). —Cory, Bds. Bahama I., p. 62 (1880). *Sylvia magnolia.* Wils., Am. Orn., III. p. 63 (1811). *Winter Plumage, Male.—* Underparts, bright yellow, streaked with black on the flanks; head and neck, ashy gray; back, yellowish olive; rump, yellow; eyelids, dull yellow; quills and tail, black, the latter having a patch of white on the inner webs of all except the two central feathers; wing with two white bands, formed by the middle and secondary coverts. *Female.—*Similar to the male, but plumage very much duller.
Length 4.50; wing 2.30; tail 2 15; tarsus.65; bill.30.

This species is probably a rare winter visitant; a single specimen was taken at Puerto Plata, San Domingo, Dec. 14, 1882.

DENDRCECA CORONATA. *(Linn.) Motacilla coronata.* Linn., Syst. Nat., I. p. 333 (1766). *Sylvia coronata.* Lath., Ind. Orn., II. p. 538 (1790). — Wils., Am.
Orn, II. p. 138 (1810). *Sylvicola coronata.* Sv. and Rich., Faun. B. Am., II. p. 216(1831).
— Aud., Bds. N. Am., II. p. 23 (1843).
Dendroeca coronata. Bd., Bds. N. A., p. 272(1858).— March, Proc. Phil. Acad., p. 292 (1863). —Gundl., " Cab., J. f. O. , p. 326 (1861)."
— Coues, Bds. N. W., p. 57 (1874).— Bd, Bwr. and Ridgw., Hist. N. A. Bds., I. p. 227(1874). — Godman and Salvin, Biol. Centr. Amcr. Zool. Aves, Pt. VI. p. 127 (1880). —Cory, Bds. Bahama I., p. 59 (1880). —Cory, Bull. Nutt. Orn. Ciub, VI. p. 151 (1881).
Sylvia xanthopygia. "Vieill., Ois. Am. Sept., II. p. 47 (1807)." *Winter Plumage, Male.* — Above, brown, faintly streaked with black; underparts, yellowish white, streaked with dark brown upon the sides and breast; rump and crown, yellow, the latter almost concealed by the brown tips of the feathers; two distinct wing-bands and spots on the three outer tail-feathers, white. *Female.*— In winter differs but slightly from the male.
Length 5.40; wing 2.80; tail 2.20; tarsus.70; bill.40.

This species is a common winter visitant. It was very common in the neighborhood of Le Coup.

DENDRfECA DISCOLOR. *(Vicitt.) Sylvia discolor.* Vieill., Ois. Am., Sept., II. p. 37 (1807). — Lemb., Aves de Cuba, p. 32 (1850). *Sylvicola discolor.* And. , Bds. Am., II. p. 68 (1841).— Gosse, Bds. Jam., p. 159 (1847). *Mniotilta discolor.* "Gray, Gen. Bds." *Rhimanphus discolor.* "Cab., J. f. O, III. p. 474 (1855)." *Dendroeca discolor.* Bd., Bds. N. A., p. 290(1858). — Gundl., J. f. O. , p. 326 (1861). —Cones, Bds. N. W. , p. 63 (1874).—Bd. and Bvr. and Ridgw. , Hist. N. A. Bds., I. p. 276 (1874). — Godman and Salvin, Biol. Centr. Amer. Zobl. Aves, Pt. IX. p. 142 (1SS1). — Cory, Bds. Bahama I., p. 64 (1880). — Cory, Bull. Nutt. Orn. Club, VI. p. 151 (1881). *Sylvia minuia.* Wils., Am. Orn., III. p. 87 (1811). *Winter Plumage, Male.* — Above, olive green; the interscapular region with faint indications of chestnut; underparts, yellow, faintly striped with ash upon the sides; throat, yellow, showing slight traces of white; a narrow yellow stripe from the nostril, encircling the eye, broken at its posterior part by a streak of ash; quills and tail-feathers, brown, edged with white; two outer tail-feathers with a long patch of white upon the inner webs. *Winter Plumage, Female.* — Similar to the male, but the markings much paler; yellow stripe of the eye very indistinct, and of a pale yellowish white.
Length 4.50; wing 2.10; tail 2; tarsus. 74; bill.40.

This species is not uncommon during the winter months.

DENDRCECA PALMARUM, *(Cm.) Motadlla palmarum.* "Gm., Syst. Nat., I. p. 951

(1788)." *Sylvia palmarum.* Lath., Ind. Orn., II. p. 544 (1790). *Sylvicola palmarum.* Salle, P. Z. S., 1857, p. 231. *Dendraca palmarum.* Bd., Bds. N. A., p. 288 (1858). — Gund., J. f. O., p. 326 (1861). —Colics, Bds. N. W., p. 67 (1874).—Bd., Bwr. and Ridgw., Hist. N. A. Bds., I. p. 273 (1874).— Cory, Bds. Bahama I., p. 68 (1880). —Cory, Bull. Nutt. Orn. Club, VI. p. 151 (18S1).

Sylvicola pctcchia. "Sv. and Rich., Faun. B. Am., II. p. 215 (1831)." — And., Bds. Am., II. p. 55 (1841).

Winter Plumage, Male. — Above, olive brown, the feathers with darker centres, becoming olive green upon the rump; crown of the head showing indistinct trace of chestnut; throat and superciliary line from nostril, pale yellowish white; underparts, yellowish white, becoming brighter upon the belly, streaked with pale brown; crissum, pale yellow; outer edges of wing and tail-feathers, yellowish white; a white patch at the end of the inner webs of the two outer tailfeathers. *Winter Plumage, Female.*— Slightly smaller than the male; chestnut entirely wanting upon the crown; throat more of a brownish cast, and general plumage slightly darker.

Length 4.85; wing 2.45; tail 2.20; tarsus.78; bill.40.

The present species is a common winter visitant.

. DENDRCECA PINUS. *(Wits.) Sylvia pinus.* Wils., Am. Orn., III. p. 25 (1811). *Sylvicola pinus.* "Jard., Rich, and Bp., Lists."—Aud., Bds. Am., II. p. 37 (1841). *Dendrceca pinus.* Bd., Bds. N. Am., p. 277 (1858). — Coues, Bds. N. W., p. 69 (1874). —Bd., Bwr. and Ridgw., Hist. N. A. Bds., I. p. 268 (1874). — Cory, Bds. Bahama I., p. 69 (1880). — Cory, Bull. Nutt. Orn. Club, VI. p. 151 (1881). *Sylvia vigorsii.* "Aud., Orn. Biog., I. p. 153 (1832)." *Vireo vigorsii.* Nutt., Man., I. p. 318 (1832).

Winter Plumage, Male. — Above, olive green; a yellow superciliary line from the base of the bill; underparts, with the exception of the belly, bright yellow; the sides of the breast with indistinct streaks of olive; sides of the head, olive green; belly and crissum, dusky white; wings and tail, dark brown, the feathers edged with dusky white, the former showing two distinct bands; inner webs of the two outer tail-feathers showing oblique patches of dull white.

Winter Plumage, Female. — Smaller than the male, and much paler; upper parts, grayish, with trace of olive; throat, very pale yellow, becoming grayish brown upon the sides of the belly; side of the head and neck, gray.

Length 5.50; wing 2.80; tail 2.35; tarsus.80; bill.50.

This Warbler is a winter visitant, and may, perhaps, be considered a resident. That it breeds in San Domingo occasionally there can be no doubt, as several specimens of young birds were taken in July, near La Vega.

Subfamily, GEOTH LYPIN/E.

Gents: SKU'IU.'S. Swaix. *si-:Irnl"s. Sivawsox, Zool. Journ., ///. /.* 171, 1827. SEIURUS AUROCAPILLUS. *(Linn.) Motacilla aurocapilla.* Linn., Syst. Nat., I. p. 334 (1766). *Turdus aurocapillus.* Lath., Ind. Orn., II. p 328 (1790).— Wils., Am. Orn., III. p. 88 (1810). — Aud., Orn. Biog., II. p. 253 (1834). *Sciurus aurocapillus.* Sv., Zool. Journ., III. p. 171 (1827). — "Aud., Bds. Am., III. p. 35."— Bd., B. N. A., p. 260 (1858). — Gosse, Bds. Jam., p. 152 (1847). —Coucs, Bds. N. W., p. 70 (1874). — Bd., Bwr. and Ridgw., Hist. N. A. Bds., I. p. 280 (1874).— Godman and Salvin, Biol. Centr. Amer. Zool. Aves, Pt. IX. p. 144 (1881).— Cory, Bds. Bahama I., p. 70 (1880). — Cory, Bull. Nutt. Orn. Club, VI. p. 151 (1881). *Henicocichla aurocappa.* "Cab., Gundl., J. f. O., p. 326 (1861)." *Turdus coronatus.* "Vieill., Ois. Am., Sept. II. p. 8 (1807)."

Winter Plumage, Male. — Above, olive green; crown, brownish orange, bordered by two black streaks from base of the bill to nape; underparts, white, with an olive tint upon the sides; breast and sides of the belly streaked with dark brown; crissum, white; legs, pale flesh color.

The female does not differ from the male.

Length 5.80; wing 3.05; tail 2.30; tarsus.90; bill.58.

This species is common during the winter. We found it abundant in the woods back of Gonaives and Jacmel.

SEIURUS MOTACILLA. *(Vicitt. Turdus motacilla.* Vieill., Ois. Am., Sept. II. p. 9 (1807). *Henicocichla motacilla.* Cab., J. f. O., p. 240 (1857). *Seiurus motacilla.* "Bp., Consp. Av., I. 306 (1850)." *Siurus motacilla.* Coues, Bull. Nutt. Orn. Club, II. p. 33 (1877).— Coues, Bds. Colora. Vail., p. 299 (1878). — Godman and Salvin, Biol. Centr. Amer. Zool. Aves, Pt. IX. p. 147 (1881). *Seiurus ludoviciam1s.* "Bp., List, 1838." — Bd.,. Bds. N. A., p. 262 (1858). —Bd., Rev., p. 217 (1864). —Coues, Bds. N. W., p. 72 (1874). —Cory, Bull. Nutt. Orn. Club, VI. p. 151 (1881).—Bd., Bwr. and Ridgw., Hist. N. A. Bds., I. p. 287 (1874). *Henicocichla ludoviciana.* "Scl., Cat., p. 25 (1862)." *Sp. Char., Male.* — Above, dark olive brown; a white superciliary line from the base of the mandible to the nape, crossing the upper lid; underparts, white, with a shade of buff on the flanks and tail coverts; a distinct maxillary line; breast and sides of the body with arrowshaped markings of dusky brown; some specimens show the spots on the throat.

The sexes are similar.

Length 6; wing 3.25; tail 2.30; tarsus. 80; bill.50.

The present species is a resident in San Domingo, although its numbers are probably augmented by migrants from the United States in winter.

Five specimens are before me, which are as follows: —

Bds. N. W., p. 74 (1874). —Bd., Bwr. and Ridgw., Hist. N. A. Bds., I. p. 297 (1874). — Godman and Salvin, Biol. Centr. Amer. Zool. Aves, Pt. IX. p. 150 (1SS1). — Cory, Bds. Bahama I., p. 72 (1880). —Cory, Bull. Nutt. Orn. Club, VI. p. 151 (1S81). *Sylvia marilandica.* "Wils., Am. Orn., I. p. 88 (1808)." *Trichas marilandica.* "Bp.,

List, 1838. — Consp. Av., I. p. 310 (1850)." —Aud., Syn., p. 65 (1839). — Aud., Bds. Am., II. p. 78 (1841). *Sylvia roscoc.* "Aud., Orn. Biog., I. p. 124 (1832)."
Trichas roscoe. "Nutt., Man., I., 2d Ed., p. 457 (1840)."
Winter Plumage,.Iale.— Upper parts, olive green; throat, bright yellow, becoming greenish upon the belly and olive upon the sides; a broad black line passing from the sides of the neck through the eye and over the forehead, with a suffusion of gray behind it upon the crown and faintly visible along its upper edge; crissum, pale yellow; wings and tail, olive green, the former showing a yellow line upon the carpus. Some 'birds show a slight tinge of brown upon the head. *Winter Ph1magc, Female.*— Pale olive above and yellowish below; no black on the head. , Length 4.60; wing 2.20; tail 2.25; tarsus.80; bill.40. .;i
This species is common in winter, frequenting the thickets and low ground.
"$? Genus: LIGIA. Cory.
LIGEA: CORY, AUK, I. p. I, 1884.
LIGEA PALUSTRIS. *Cory.*
Ligca palustris. Cory, Auk, I. p I, pi. 1 (1884).
Sp. Char., Afale. — Crown, nape, and upper portion of back, slaty plumbeous; rest of back and upper surface of wings and tail, yellowish green; throat, breast, and sides, grayish plumbeous, showing a dull olive tinge on
O - the sides, darkest on the flanks; the middle of the throat showing a slight grayish tinge, and the middle of the belly showing distinctly white; outer webs of primaries and most of the secondaries, yellowish green, giving the wing a general greenish appearance; inner webs of primaries, dark brown, apparently slate color in some lights; under surface of tail, dull green; eyelids, white.
Length 5.50; wing 2.50; tail 2.50; tarsus.75; bill.50; mid-toe.40. *Female.* — General appearance of the male, but differs from it by underparts being tinged with olive, mixing with the gray, and top of the head green, showing the slate color faintly.

Subfamily, SETOPH A GIN.
Genus: SETOPHAGA. Swain.
SETOniAGA: SIVAINSOX,. ZOOl.. JOl'R.V., III. p. 360, 1827.
SETOPHAGA RUTICILLA. *(Linn.) Muscicapa ruticilla.* Linn., Syst. Nat., I. p. 326 (1766).— Wils., Am. Orn., I. p. 103 (1808).— Aud, Bds. Am., I. p. 240, pi. 68. *Setophaga ruticilla.* Sv., "Phil. Mag. , new sen, I. p. 368."—Coues, Key, p. 110 (1872). —Coues, Bds. N. W., p. 81 (1874).—Bd., Bvr. and Ridgw., Hist. N. A. Bds., I. p. 322 (1874). — Godman and Salvin, Biol. Centr. Amer. Zool. Aves, Pt. IX. p. 178 (1881). —Cory, Bds. Bahama I., p. 75 (1880). —Cory, Bull. Nutt. Orn. Club, VI. p. 151 (1sS1). *Sylvania ruticilla.* "Nutt., Man., I. p. 291 (1832)." *Motacilla flavicauda.* "Gm., Syst. Nat., I. 997, 1788 (9)." *Winter Plumage, Male.* — Upper parts and throat, black; belly, white, slightly tinged with orange; wings, black, with a broad band of orange: basal half of the tail-feathers, except the middle ones, and a patch on each side of the breast, orange red. *Winter Plumage, Female.* — Black, replaced by olive green; an ashy appearance upon the head; the orange red replaced by pale i yellow.
Length 5.20; wing 2.45; tail 2.38; tarsus.70; bill.18.
The Redstart is a common winter visitant.
FAMILY CCEREBID:.
Subfamily, CCEREBIN/E.
Genus: CERTHIOLA. Sund. *CERTHIOLA: SUXDEVALL, OFVERS VET. AKAD. HANDL., p.* 99, 1835, *STOCKHOLM.* CERTHIOLA BANANIVORA. *(Cm.) Motacilla bananivora.* Gmelin, Syst. Nat., I. p. 951 (1/SS).
Suerier (?) (de St. Dominique). "Buff., Hist. Nat. Ois., V. p. 545 (1778)."
Certhiola clusia. "Herz. v. Wiirttcmb. Hartl. Naumannia, II. Heft. 2, p. 56 (1852) *(sine desery* — Finsch, Verhandl. Zool. Bot.
Gesell, XXI. p. 771 (1871). — Sclat. and Salv., Nomen. Avi.
Neot., p. 17 (1873). *Certhiola clucia.* Cory, Bull. Nutt. Orn. Club, VI. p. 151 (1881).
Certhiola (?). Salle (Sclater), P. Z. S., 1857, p. 233. *Certhiola bananivora.* Bd.

, Bwr. and Ridgw., Hist. N. A. Bds., I. p. 427 (1874).— Bryant, Proc. Boston Soc. Nat. Hist., XI. p. 95 (1866). *Male.*— Upper surface, including head, cheek, wings, and tail, dull black; a superciliary white stripe extending from the base of the upper mandible to the nape; throat, dark slate color; underparts, bright yellow, becoming grayish olive upon the sides and thighs; rump, bright yellow; carpus, bright yellow; an edging of white upon the basal portion of primaries on the outer webs, very narrow upon the first, the whole nearly concealed by the coverts, forming a narrow white wing-band; bill and feet, black; tail slightly tipped with dull white on the outer feathers.
The sexes are similar.
Length 4.40; wing 2.40; tail 1.60; tarsus.60; bill.50.
This little Creeper is abundant in some localities among the mountains. At Petion Ville (Le Coup) we observed it daily, running about the trunks of the banana-trees. Very few were seen in the low land of the interior.
A nest of this species, taken May 1, 1883, contained two fresh eggs. It was built on the end of a long limb in deep woods. It is very large for the size of the bird, and has a passageway or hole leading to the interior sufficiently long to entirely conceal the female during the period of incubation. The eggs are dull white, thickly mottled, and lined with brown, heaviest on the larger end. They measure 1700-*X* /' inches.
No. Date. Sex. Mus. Locality. Length. Wing. Tail. Tarsus.
., T, _ (Sanlana,) 3743 bept. 1, 1883. g C. B. C. San Domingo, f 4.4 2.40 l'6 .6o 1193 Feb. 15, 18S1. 9 C. B. C. LCji(ai't"P' 3-8o 2.25 1.45.Co 1186 March 4, 1831. $ C. B. C. auT 4. 2.4 145 '-6o 1188 March 9,1881. $ C. B. C. I'llliti"P' 4. 2.40 'S.6o
I439 Feb. 28, 1881. 3 C. B. C. j aid!''' 4-2-40 1.45-60 3744 Sept. 3,1883. 9 C. B. C. , Sanlana' *I* 2.45 1.45.58 (San Dunungo. J FAMILY HIRUNDINID/E.
Subfamily, H I RU ND I N I N/E.
Genus: PROGNE. Boie.
PROGNE: BOIE., ISIS, 971, 1826.
PROGNE DOMINICENSIS. *(Cm.) Hirundo*

domiuiccnsis. Gm., Syst. Nat., I. p. 1025 (1788). *Hirnndellc de S. Domingue.* "Briss., Orn., II. 493, n. 3 (1760)." *Prague dominicensis.* Boie., Isis, p. 971 (1826). — Gosse, Bds. Jam., p. 69 (1847).—Bd., Bwr-and Ridgv., Hist. N. A. Bds., I. p. 328 (1874). —Coues, Bds. Col. Val., p. 446 (1878). *Sp. Char., Male.* — Entire upper surface, throat, and sides, steel blue, showing purplish reflections in some lights; rest of underparts, white; quills and tail, dark brown, the feathers having a faint bluish tinge on the outer webs; bill and feet, black. *Sp. Char., Female.*— Upper surface as in the male; throat and sides, ashy brown; otherwise resembling the male. Length 7; wing 5.60; tail 3.10; tarsus. 50; bill.50.

The present species was not uncommon near Samana. None were taken elsewhere, although it is probably abundant in some localities.

Genus: HIRUNDO. Li.vn.

HIRUNDO: LINN., SYST. NAT., 7, loIIi I'.d. , p. 191, 1758.

HIRUNDO SCLATERI. *Cory. Hirundo sclateri.* Cory, Auk, I. p. 2 (1884). *Hirundo euchrysea (var. dominiccnsis?).* Bryant, Proc. Bost. Soc. Nat. Hist. , XI. p. 95 (1866). *Sp. Char., Male.* — Above, bright bluish green, showing a golden color in some lights, becoming decidedly blue on the forehead; upper surface of wings and tail showing a tinge of dull blue, brightest on the tail; underparts, pure white; primaries, brown; bill and legs, very dark brown. The sexes are similar.

Length 5; wing 4.60; tail 2.

The present species differs decidedly from *Hirundo eucilrysca,* from Jamaica, that species having the upper parts bright golden green, and lacking the blue on the forehead entirely. The San Domingo bird is also larger, and the bill apparently somewhat more slender.

Dr. Bryant mentions the present bird in his list as *//. euchrysca (var. dominicensis?),* stating that on account of its smaller bill it might be a variety; but he gives no description by which it could be identified.

This species was quite abundant in the vicinity of La Vega, San Domingo, during July and August; none were taken elsewhere, although a small flock of swallows were observed a few miles east of Gonaives, which I believe were the present species.

No. Date. Sex. Mus. Locality. Length. Wing. Tail.
3446 Aug. 2,,883. C.B.C. SanDiingo. 5-4-6o 2. 3447 July 28,1883. g C.B.C S;ll;a)ola J 47S 4.40 2.20 3445 Aug. 2,,883. g C.B.C. sj,. j 5-47 2.20 344, Aug. 2,1883. $ C-B-C- Sanliningo. J 46 4 S 2.' 3434 Aug. 1.,883. $ C-B-C- SanDomfngo. J S'' 4 S 2-20 3428 Aug. 1, 1883. S C. B. C. sjSfga 4." 4-ao 2. 05 3448 Aug.,,,,883. $ C. B. C. sa V J,._ 3453 Aug.,,,,883. tM- SalSngo. 4.5 a.1S 3449 Aug. 1,1883. i C-B-C SanDommgo.! 4.8 4.40 *2TM PETROCHELIDOX: CABANIS, MUS. HEIN.,* 1850-1, *p.* 47. PETROCHELIDON FULVA. *(Viciit.) Hirundo fulva.* Viciil., Ois. Am., Sept. I. p. 62, 1807. *Petrochelidon fulva.* Cab., Mus. Hein., p. 47 (1850). — Gundl., J. f. (3. , 1856, p. 3. — "Bd, Rev. Am. Eds., p. 291 (1874)."— Coues, Bds. Col. Val, p. 426 (1878). — Cory, Bull. Nutt Orn. Club, VI. p. 152 (1881). *Sp. Char., Male.* — Throat and sides of the breast, pale rufous brown, the color passing around the neck in a narrow line at the nape; belly and crissum, dull white, the latter showing a rufous tinge; top of the head, bluish black, the color nearly encircling the eye; forehead and rump, dark rufous brown; back, bluish black, streaked with white; wings and tail, dark brown; bill and feet, black.

The sexes are apparently similar.

Length 4.70; wing 4; tail 1.85; tarsus. 40; bill.27.

This Swallow does not appear to be very abundant in San Domingo; only a few flocks were seen, and but two specimens taken. At Gonaives, on the day of our arrival, several flocks were observed flying about the houses, but the next day none were to be seen.

No. Date. Sex. Mus. Locality. Length. Wing. Tail. Tarsus.
re T u /-u / (Gonaives, 1466 rob. 10, 1881. $? C, B. C. H-Y t '7 4" 5 ' ,, T1,, (Almercen,) 3518 Aug.,1,1883. 9 C-B-C San Domingo. S ' & FAMILY

Subfamily, VIREONINE.

Genus: VIREO. Vieill.

VIREO: VIEILLOT, OIS. AM., SEPT. I. p. 83, 1807.

VIREO CALIDRIS. *(Linn.) Motacilla calidris.* "Linn, Syst. Nat., loth Ed., p. 184 (1758)."

Muscicapa altiloqua. Vieill., Ois. Am., Sept. I. p. 67 (1807).

Vireo altiloqua. Gray, Genera. — Salle (Sclater), P. Z. S., 1857,

p. 231. — March, Pr. Acad. N. Sc., 1863, p. 294. *Vircosylvia olivacea.* Gosse, Bds. Jam., p. 194 (1847). *Vireosylvia calidris.* Bd., Rev., p. 329 (1874). *Vireo calidris.* Bryant, Pr. Bost. Soc. Nat. Hist., XI. p. 93 (1866) *Vireo altiloquus barbatulus.* Cab. — Cory, Bull. Nutt. Orn. Club, VI. p. 152 (1881). *Sp. Char., Male.* — Crown, grayish, but showing a slight olive tinge; upper parts, dull olive green; a buff superciliary line and a dusky stripe through the eye; a narrow dusky maxillary line halfway down the sides of the throat; sides, pale yellowish olive; lining of wings and under tail coverts, pale yellow; tail, olive.

The sexes are similar.

Length 5.80; wing 3.20; tail 2.50; tarsus.68; bill.60.

FAMILY AMPELIDE.

Subfamily, MYIADESTINE.

Genus: DULUS. Vieill.

DULUS: VIEILLOT, ANALYSE, p. 42, *No. ly,* 1816.

DULUS DOMINICUS. *(Linn.) Tanagra dominica.* Linn., Syst. Nat., I. p. 316 (1766). *Dulus dominicus.* Strickl., Cont. Orn., p. 103 (1851). — " Lafr., Rev. Mag., 583 (1851)."—Bd., Rev. Am. Bds., p. 403 (1874).— Salle (Sclater), P. Z. S., 1857, p. 231.— Cory, Bull. Nutt. Orn. Club, VI. p. 152 (1881). *Dulus palmarum.* "Vieill., Nouv. Diet., X. 438 (1817)." *Sp. Char., Male.* — Above, dull olive brown; throat, dull white; feathers of the throat and underparts, dark brown in the centre, broadly edged with dull rufous white, giving the bird a heavily streaked appearance; rump, green; primaries and secondaries, dark brown, the outer webs edged with green, the inner webs becoming very pale on the edges; tail, dark brown, the feathers very narrowly edged with green; iris, orange.

The sexes are similar.

Length 6.20; wing 3.50; tail 3.10; tarsus.80; bill.55.

A gregarious species, abundant among the mountains; usually in the vicinity of cocoanut-trees. The food consists of insects of various kinds, and fruit in the season.

No. Pate. Sex. Mus. Locality. Length. Wing. Tail. Tarsus.
3377 Sept. 10,,883. S C. B. C. SanS Domingo. 6'20 3'5 3'10 '8o Genus: MYIADESTES. Swain.

MYIADESTES: SWAINSOff, NAT. LIBR. ORNITH., X. p. 132, 1838.

MYIADESTES MONTANUS. Cory. *Myiadestes montanus.* Cory, Bull. Nutt. Orn. Club, VI. pp. 130, 151 (1881). *Myiadcctes montauus.* Sharpe, Cat. Bds. Brit. Mus., VI. p. 370 (1881). *Myadestes montanus.* Stcjneger, Pr. Nat. Mus., V. p. 23 (1882). *Sp. Char., Female.* — Upper parts and two central tail-feathers, slaty gray; primaries and secondaries, brownish black, showing white near the base of the inner webs; outer webs of primaries and terminal portion of the outer webs of secondaries, edged with gray; no white spot on the chin; throat, crissum, and belly, near the vent, reddish brown, intermediate between that of *M. solitarius* and *M. sibilans,* but approaching nearer the color of the former; rest of underparts, pale gray; outer tail-feather, white, with black shaft, showing a dark tinge near the extremity of the outer web; second feather, black, with the central portion of the terminal half, white, the black narrowing to the extremity, leaving the tip white; third feather showing a triangular patch of white at the tip; rest of tailfeathers, except the two central ones, black; bill, black; legs and feet, pale; iris, brown.
Length 7; wing 3.35; tail 3.38; tarsus 1; bill.38.

The only example of this bird yet taken is the type specimen described above, which was procured in the neighborhood of Fort Jacque, Haiti. It is apparently rare, frequenting the summits of the highest mountains. The natives call it "Musician," and have a variety of opinions concerning it. It is generally thought to be a spirit, which, if seen, would bring misfortune to the person who was so unfortunate as to meet with it.

No. Date. Sex. Mus. Locality. Length. Wing. Tail. Tarsus.
1253 March3,1881. 9 ad. C. B. C. j FHUe' 7-3-35 3-38 1. Genus: SPINDALIS. Jard.

SPINDALIS: JARD. AND SELBY, "ILL. OR. V., IV. S., 1836."

SPINDALIS MULTICOLOR. (*Vicitt. Tanagra multicolor.* Vieill., Enc. Meth., p. 776; Gal. Ois., I. p. 100, pi. 76. *Spindalis multicolor.* Bp., Consp., p. 240 (1850). — Scl., P. Z. S., 1856, p. 230. — Salle, P. Z. S., 1857, p. 231. — Cory, Bull. Nutt. Orn. Club, VI. p. 152 (1881). *Tanagra dominicensis.* Bryant, Pr. Bost. Soc. Nat. Hist., XI. p. 92 (1868).

Sp. Char., Male. — Head, black; a superciliary stripe from the forehead to the nape; a broad stripe of black from the bill, through the eye, to the neck; chin, white, the white extending in a stripe below the black of the cheek to the neck; rest of throat black, with a yellow stripe in the centre, reaching the white of the chin; breast, chestnut, shading into yellow upon the underparts and sides; a collar of bright orange yellow upon the nape, joining the white stripe of the throat; back, olive; rump, chestnut; abdomen and crissum, white; tail, brownish black; the inner webs of the two outer tail-feathers broadly marked with white; wings, dark brown, with white edgings to the coverts and secondaries; lesser wing coverts, chestnut; bill and feet, bluish black.

I unfortunately do not possess a female example of this species; but it somewhat resembles the female 6". *portoricensis,* being a dull gray-colored bird, showing olive on the back and a yellowish cast on the rump; the undcrparts grayish, whitening at the vent.

Length 6.40; wing 3.35; tail 3.10; tarsus.75; bill.40.

The present species is very rare, and comparatively nothing is known regarding it. Salle states that it is rare, and frequenting the high trees of the valleys among the mountains in the interior of the island. He states that it has an agreeable songv The specimens which I possess are as follows: —

No. Date. Sex. Mus. Locality. Length. Wing. Tail. Tarsus.
1250 March 3, 1881. $ C. B. C. j Si!'''
6'40 3.35 3.'o.75 1251 March 3, 1881. $ C. B. C. j LHaiti!P' 6"K 3.35 3.15-75 4260 Dec.,,,88,,. C. B. C. j go. 3.5 3-. 75 r *Sp. Char., Male.*— Top of the head and cheeks, black; a spot of white on each side of the forehead; a white stripe touching the upper eyelid, commencing at the centre of the eye, passing backward on the head; a patch of white on the lower eyelid; a gray collar on the nape, extending upon and joining the gray of ftf.' the sides; sides, slaty gray; throat, white, the white extending in *Kb* a narrow line down the middle of belly to the vent; the back, rump, tail, outer webs of secondaries, and coverts, bright yellowish green; quills, brown; bill and feet, bluish black. -- *tL K-P-*

Length 6.70; wing 3.70; tail 3; tarsus. 85; bill.70.

The sexes are similar.

The present species is very abundant among the mountains of the interior and in some localities on the coast. None were observed at Jacmel, on the south side of the island, although it is probably to be found there. It resembles a Vireo somewhat in its habits and is very tame and unsuspicious. The note is a short, sharp "chip," usually uttered when in the act of taking flight. The food consists of insects and fruit of various kinds.

i PHOENICOPHILUS DOMINICENSIS. Cory. *Phcenicophilus dominicensis.* Cory, Bull. Nutt. Orn. Club, VI. p.
129 (18S1).

Sp. Char., Male. — Forehead and sides of the head, black; a spot of white above and below the eye, and on each side of the forehead; chin, white, extending in two stripes down the sides of the throat to the breast, bordering the black of the head; the rest of the head, neck, and underparts, grayish plumbeous; back, wing coverts, tail and coverts, and outer edges of wing-feathers, bright yellowish green; inner webs of primaries and secondaries, brown, pale on the edges; legs and lower mandible, dark slate color; upper mandible, black; iris, reddish brown.

Length 6.80; wing 3.50; tail 2.30; tarsus.82; bill.68.

The sexes are similar.

The present species seems to be restricted to the west coast, all the specimens were procured in the vicinity of Jacmel. Authors have generally considered this bird to be the female of *P. palmarum;* but a careful examination of a large series of the latter species proved conclusively the sexual difference, if any, to be merely a slight variation in size.

No. Date. Sex. Mus. Locality. Length. Wing. Tail. Tarsus.
1258 Jan. 13,1881. g C. B.C. Jc' J 6.80 3.50 2.30.82 1231 Jan. 19,1881. g C.B.C. JjgJ?1' 6.45 3.ss .18 .78
1226 Jan. 19,1881. 9 C.B.C. Jgjjjj' 6.45 3.50 2.20.80
4261 Jan. 23,1881. 9 C.B.C. j JjgJjJ-J 6.50 3.55 2.22.80

Genus: CALYPTOPHILUS.

THE AUK, I. p. 1, 1884.

CALYPTOPHILUS. *Cory.*

The present genus has the general appearance, at first glance, of *Phxnicophitus,* but it is easily separated from it by the following characters:— *a.* Tail short, about four fifths as long as the wing; middle toe about two thirds of tarsus; tail square, slightly emarginate.. .. *Phanicophtlus. b.* Tail long, equal to wing; middle toe about five sixths of tarsus; tail rounded, and strongly graduated; bill much narrower, and the legs and feet larger than in *Phxnicophilus Calyptophilus.* CALYPTOPHILUS FRUGIVORUS. *Cory. Phcenicophilus frugivorus.* Cory, Journ. Boston Zool. Soc., II. No. 4, p. 45 (1883). *Calyptophilus frugivorus.* Cory, The Auk, I. p. 3, (1884).

Sp. Char., Male. — Top of the head brown, shading into ashy on the neck behind the eye; rest of upper parts, including back and upper surface of wings and tail, brownish olive; throat, white; breast, white, becoming ashy upon the sides; flanks, brownish olive, the olive mixing with white upon the crissum; primaries I and secondaries, olive brown, the inner webs edged with very pale brown; a patch of bright yellow under the base of the wing, extending upon the carpus; eye encircled by a very narrow line of bright yellow, and a spot of yellow in front of the eye at the base of 'the mandible; upper mandible, dark brown; lower mandible, yellowish brown, darkest at the base. Some specimens show a spot of yellow upon the middle of the breast, but it is not constant. In a series of fourteen specimens, it is wanting in all but five.

The female is perhaps somewhat duller, and some specimens appear slightly smaller, but otherwise resembles the male.

Length 7.50; wing 3.70; tail 3.70; tarsus 1; toe.82; bill.75.

The present species is not common. All the specimens were taken in the swamps near Almercen, and none were observed elsewhere. It is very retiring in its habits, generally keeping concealed in the thickest and most impenetrable thickets. The note somewhat resembles that of *Phoenicophilus palmarum.*

Subfamily, EUPHONIN.

Genus: EUPHONIA. Desm.

EUPHONIA: DESMAREST, HIST. NAT. DES. TANGARAS, ETC, f) (1805).

EUPHONIA MUSICA. *Cm. L'Organiste dc S. Dominge.* "Buff., Pl. Enl. 809, Fig. 1. " *Pipra musica.* Gm., Syst. Nat., I. 1004 (1788). *Tanagra musica.* "Vieill., Enc. Meth., p. 787." *Euphonia musica.* Gray, Gen., p. 367. — Bonap., Consp., p. 232 (1850). —Sclater, P. Z. S., 1856, p. 271. —Salle (Sclater), P. Z. S., 1857, p. 231. — Bryant, Proc. Boston Soc. Nat. Hist., XI. p. 92 (1866). —Cory, Bull. Nutt. Orn. Club, VI. p. 152(1881). *Euphone musica.* Lembeye, Aves de Cuba, p. 42 (1850). *f Sp. Char., Male.* — Crown, light blue, the color extending upon the nape, and slightly upon the sides of the neck; forehead, underparts, and rump, brownish orange; throat, cheeks, back and tail, bluish black, showing purple reflections; the purple very prominent on the back; a line of purplish black separating the blue and orange of the head and forehead; primaries, dark brown, becoming pale on the edges of the inner webs; bill and feet, black. *Sp. Char., Female.*— Underparts, yellowish green, becoming yellowish on the throat; cheeks and line above the forehead, dull black; head and nape extending upon the sides of the neck, light blue; forehead, orange brown; back, rump, and wing coverts, olive green; tail, dull black, showing a tinge of green upon the feathers; primaries as in the male, except showing an almost indistinct greenish edging upon the outer webs.

Length 4.40; wing 2.60; tail 1.80; tarsus.50; bill.25.

Immature Male. — Forehead, pale orange; top of the head, grayish blue; back, olive green, blotched with dark blue; rump, brownish orange; wings and tail, black, some of the tertiaries and coverts edged with olive green; underparts, olive green, marked with brownish on the throat; dark orange, shaded with greenish, on the belly and crissum; bill and feet, black.

This pretty little species seems to be rare even in San Domingo. Generally found in pairs, they frequent the highest branches of large trees. The period of incubation probably occurs in January, as young birds were taken in March and April. The food consists of insects, berries, and small seeds.

The following measurements are from a series of specimens in my collection: —

No. Date. Sex. Mus. Locality. Length. Wing. Tail. Tarsus.
3377 Aug. 14, 1883. *i* C-B'C- SanSngo. ' 2.5 '.5 3376 Aug.,5,1883. S C-B'C-saDomlngo. 4.9 ' 3380 Aug. 6,1883. S C.B.C. Sanefn'go. 4-10 2.50 1.50.60 3382 Aug. 12,I883. S C.B.C. SaD'go. 4-09 2-48 1.48.60 3383 Sept. 7,,883. S C.B.C. jaTMTM;go j 4.12 2.5o,.5,.60 3381 Aug. 6,1883. C.B.C. SaDS'go. 4-05-45-So-62 Genus: PHONIPARA. Bonap.

PffOMPARA: BONAPARTE, CONSPECTUS, p. 494, 1850.

PHONIPARA ZENA. *(Linn.) Fringilla zena.* Linn., Syst. Nat., I. 10 ed. p. 183 (1758).

Fringilla bicolor. Linn., Syst. Nat., I. 12 ed. p. 324 (1766).

Spermophila bicolor. Gosse, Bds. Jam., p. 252 (1847). — Bryant, List Bds. Bahama Iids., 1859.
Phonipara marchi. Bd., Pr. A. N. Soc., Phila., 1863, p. 297. *Fringilla zena var. marchi.* Bryant, Pr. Bost. Soc. Nat. Hist. , 1867,
P-43 *Fringilla (Phonipara) zena var. portoricencis.* Bryant, Pr. Bost. Soc. Nat. Hist., X. p. 254 (1865).
Phonipara bicolor. Scl., Cat. Am. Bds. , p. 106 (1862). — Bp., Consp., p. 494 (1850). — A. & E. Newton, Ibis, 1859, pp. 147, 376. — Cory, Bds. Bahama I., p. 91 (1880). — Cory, Bull. Nutt. Orn. Club, VI. p. 152 (1881). *Phonipara zcna.* Bd., Bwr. & Ridgw., N. Am. Bds., II. p. 93 (1874). *Eucthia bicolor.* Gund., Anal, de la Soc. Esp. de Hist. Nat., Tomo VII. p. 205 (1878). *Sp. Char., Male.* — General plumage, dull olive; whole of breast and throat, black; a blackish tinge sometimes perceptible on the forehead; belly, dull gray, shading into olive on the flanks; surface of wings and tail, olive; primaries, secondaries, and tail-feathers, brown, showing olive on the outer webs; some males only have a small patch on the chin black, others have nearly the entire under surface black, the extent of the color varying greatly, perhaps according to the age of the bird. *Sp. Char., Female.* — Resembles the male, but lacking the black of the throat, which is replaced by dull olivaceous gray.

Length 4.10; wing 2.05; tail 1.60; tarsus.54; bill.40.

A very abundant species, seeming to prefer the neighborhood of towns and villages, and is generally the first bird to be seen on landing at any of the seaports. The note is a short, sharp "chip," uttered while perched or fluttering among the bushes. Its food consists of insects, berries, and often fruit of various kinds.

No. Date. Sex. Mus. Locality. Length. Wing. Tail. Tarsus.
3760 Sept. 4,1883. C.B.C. SaSTM£go. 4-10 2.oS,.60.54 376, Sept. 4,,883. 9 C. B.C. J-go. 4.` " ` `« PHONIPARA OLIVACEA. (Cm.) *Emberiza olivacea.* Gmelin., Syst. Nat., I. p. 309 (1788). *Spermopkila olivacea.* Gosse, Bds. Jam.

, p. 249 (1847). *Phonipara olivacea.* Scl., P. Z. S., 1855, p. 159. — Salle, P. Z. S., 1857, p. 232. — Scl., Cat. Am. Bds., p. 107 (1862). — Cory, Bull. Nutt. Orn. Club, VI. p. 152 (1881). *Fringilla (Phonipara) olivacea.* Bryant, Pr. Bost. Soc. Nat. Hist., XI. p. 93 (1866). *Eucthia Icpida.* Gund., Anal, de la Soc. Esp. de Hist. Nat., Tomo VII. p. 204 (1878).
Sp. Char., Male. — Above, dull olive; a superciliary stripe, and a patch on the chin, and upper throat orange yellow, rest of throat black; a narrow line of black bordering the yellow of the throat, reaching to front of eye; lower eyelid, dull yellow; underparts, olivaceous gray; carpus, dull yellow; bill and feet, dark brown. *Sp. Char., Female.* — Lacking the black of head and throat in the male; the yellow is much less conspicuous and paler; belly, dull gray; the olive of the back, duller than in the male.

Length 4; wing 2; tail 1.50; tarsus.50; bill.30.

Although not as abundant as the preceding species, the Finch is common in some localities. About Le Coup we saw it every day, and procured many specimens. The note is a clear trill, which is very pleasing. Its habits and food seem identical with *P. zena.* A nest of the species, taken Aug. 15, contained two eggs which were quite fresh. They are dull white, heavily blotched with brown on the larger end, and faintly spotted all over with the same color. They measure-jV1TxiV(T inch. The nest is usually built in the branches of a low tree, and is made of grass very loosely put together.

No. Date. Sex. Mus. Locality. Length. Wing. Tail. Tarsus.
3657 July 24, 1883. C-B-C- San D?nfin'go. 4-»-'.5.5 3659 July 35, 1833. 9 C.B.C. SJS. 4-1.95-48.5o FAMILY FRINGILLID:.
Subfamily, FRI NGI L LI Genus: LOXIMITRIS. Bryant.
LOXIMITRIS: BRYANT, PR. BOST. SOC. NAT. HIST., XI. p. 93, 1866.
LOXIMITRIS DOMINICENSIS. Bryant. *Chrysomitris (Loximitris) dominicerisis.* Bryant, Pr. Bost. Soc. Nat.

Hist., XI. p. 93 (1866). *Chrysomitris dominicensis.* Cory, Bull. Nutt. Orn. Club, VI. p. 152 (1881).
Sp. Char., Male. — " Bill, light brown color, with the top dusky; whole head and throat, black; back and scapulars, olive; the centre of each feather dusky; upper tail coverts, bright olive yellow; wings, with the quills and coverts, blackish brown; the smaller coverts with so much of the tips olive as to appear almost wholly of this color; the greater coverts and all the quill-feathers, except the first, bordered externally with the same color, very narrowly on the primaries, and suddenly wider on the secondaries, but only on the posterior half, so that the closed wing presents a distinct blackish bar, running nearly across its centre; tail with the centre feather, outer web of first, and tips of all, blackish brown, the rest bright chrome yellow; beneath yellow, washed with olive on the flanks, and brightest on the crissum." — *Bryant, P. B. S.* (Orig. Desc.

Length 4.10; wing 2.60; tail 1.55; tarsus.53; bill.38.

This interesting species is apparently not common, although several specimens in immature plumage were procured; no adult birds were seen. It appears to be somewhat restricted in its range, as all specimens thus far have been taken in Haiti, and none have been recorded from the eastern or San Domingo part of the island. The specimen figured in the plate represents an adult bird which has been forwarded to me through the kindness of Mr. Robert Ridgway, from the Smithsonian Institution.

The specimens examined are as follows: —

No. Date. Sex. Mus. Locality. Length. Wing. Tail. Tarsus.
1220 March 2, 1881. $ yg. C. B. C. j „ '.-4.20 2.40 1.70.5 1221 March;, 1881. 9 yg. C. B. C. J LeH(Jt"P 4-2o 2.40 1. 70.5 no2 Feb. 28, 1881. 9yg. C.B.C. J LeH5t"P' 4-2.35 1.65.5 42464 June 3, 1866. 3 ad. — Port£Je' 4.10 2.60,.55.53
Subfamily, S PE RM OP H I L I Genus: LOXIGILLA. Less.
LOXIGILLA: LESSON, TRAIT& D'ORN, p.

443, 1831.

LOXIGILLA VIOLACEA. *(Linn.) Loxia violacea.* Linn., Syst. Nat., I. p. 306 (1758).
Pyrrhula violacea. Gosse, Bds. Jam., p. 254 (1847). *Loxigilla violacea.* Salle, P. Z. S., 1857, p. 231. Scl., P. Z. S., 1861. p. 74. Cat. Am. Bds., p. 102 (1862). — Cory, Bds. Bahama I., p. 85 (1880). Bull. Nutt. Orn. Club, VI. p. 152 (1881). *Loxia (Pyrrhulagrd) violacea.* Bryant, Pr. Bost. Soc. Nat. Hist., XI. p. 93 (1866). *Pyrrhulagra violacea.* Bp., Consp., p. 493 (1850). *Sp. Char., Male.* — Entire plumage black, showing a slight brownish tinge upon the quills; throat, crissum, and a crescent over the eye, reddish brown; bill and legs, black. *Sp. Char., Female.* — Upper parts, gray, with a tinge of olive green upon the back; below, ash, lightest upon the belly, showing a tinge of olive upon the breast and sides; quills with fine edgings of dull white; crissum, a crescent over the eye, and markings upon the chin, pale reddish brown, much lighter than in the male; under mandible, pale. Immature birds resemble the female.
Length 5.80; wing 3; tail 2.70; tarsus. 90; bill.50.

FAMILY
Subfamily, ICTERIN.
Genus: ICTERUS. Briss.
ICTERUS: BRISSOX, ORN., II. p. 85, 1760.
ICTERUS DOMINICENSIS. *(Linn.) Oriolus dominie en sis.* Linn., Syst. Nat., I. p. 163 (1767).
Pendulilms flavigaster. Vieill., Enc. Meth., p. 705.
Xanthornus dominiccnsis. Cab., J. f. O., 1856, p. 10.
Pendulinus hypomelas. Bp., Consp., p. 433 (1850).
Icterus dominicensis. Daud., Tr. d'Orn., p. 335. — Salle, P. Z. S., 1857, p. 232. — Scl., Cat. Am. Bds., p. 131 (1862). — Cory, Bull. Nutt. Orn. Club, VI. p. 152 (1881).
Sp. Char., Male. — General plumage, black; upper wing coverts, edge of carpus, under wing coverts, lower half of back, rump, flanks, crissum, and under tail coverts, bright yellow; outer surface of wings, black; under surface of wings showing the inner webs of the feathers pale, becoming dull white at the base; bill and legs, black. *Sp. Char., Young.* — Throat, cheeks, and a narrow superciliary stripe, black; crown, sides of the head, and breast showing a brownish tinge, rest of underparts greenish yellow; back, ashy Subfamily, QUISCALIN.
Genus: QUISCALUS. Vieill.
QUISCALUS: VIEILLOT, ANALYSE, p. 36, 1816.
QUISCALUS NIGER. *(Bodd.) Oriolus niger.* Bodd., Tab. pi. Enl., p. 31 (1783). *Quiscalus niger.* Cass., Pr. A. N. S., 1866, p. 407.— Bd., Bwr. and Ridgw., N. A. Bds., II. p. 213 (1874). *Quiscalus ater.* Baird, Bryant, Pr. Bost. Soc. Nat. Hist., XI. p. 94 (1866). —Cory, Bull. Nutt. Orn. Club, VI. p. 153 (1881). *Quiscalus barita.* Salle, P. Z. S., 1857, p. 232. *Sp. Char., Male.* — General plumage, lustrous black, showing purple when held in the light; wings and tail, black with bluish reflections; bill and feet, black.
Length 10.25; wing 5.40; tail 5; tarsus 1.30; bill 1.1o.

This species is not uncommon about the lakes and rivers of the interior of the island. At Gantier it was abundant, and several specimens were procured. It was also common in the vicinity of Puerto Plata and Samana.

No. Date. Sex. Mus. Locality. Length. Wing. Tail. Tarsus. Bill.
1263 March 7, 1881. J C. B. C.-Haiti13' , IO2S S-4 s I3 I-I 3258 April 13, 1883. S C.B. C. SanJjjjgo. j IO-25 5- 4 5. 1.30 1.1o 3172 Nov. 28,1882.? C. B. C. j Sarf Domineo I 9' 4-9 4. I'20 I'10 FAMILY CORVID/E.
Subfamily, CORVINE.
Genus: CORVUS. Linn.
CORl'CS: Zl.:V., SYST. NAT., p. 155, 1766.
CORVUS LEUCOGNAPHALUS. *Daud. Corvus leucognaphalns.* Daud., Tr. d'Orn., II. p. 231. — Salle, P. Z. S., 1857, p. 232. — Bryant, Pr. Bost. Soc. Nat. Hist.,. XI. p. 94 (1866). — Gund., Anal, de la Soc. Esp. de Hist. Nat., Tomo VII. p. 214 (1878).—Hd., Bwr. and Ridgw., N. Am. Bds., II. p. 234 (1874). —Cory, Bull. Nutt. Orn. Club, VI. p. 153 (1881). *Mierocorax Ieucognaphalus.* Sharpe, Cat. Bds. Brit. Mus. , III. p. 49 (1877) *Sp. Char.* — General plumage, black, with faint bluish and purple reflections in the light, feathers of the throat having the ends separated in hair-like filaments; basal portion of the body, feathers white; bill and legs, black.
Length 18; wing 12; tail 8; tarsus 2.20; bill 2.20.

This species is common at Gantier and at Almercen. In its habits it did not appear to differ from those of other members of its family. The note is hard and very harsh, being totally different from any other species with which I am acquainted. The flesh of this and the next species is eaten by the natives, and is considered a great delicacy.

CORVUS SOLITARIUS. *Wiirt. Corvus solitarius.* Viirt, Naumannia, II. p. 55. — Gray, Hand List
Bds., II. p. 13 (1870). *Corvus palmarum.* "Wiirt, Reis, p. 73." *Mierocorax solitarius.* Sharpe, Cat. Bds. Brit. Mus., III. p. 49 (1877).
Sp. Char. — General plumage, black, with a purple gloss to the feathers; coverts and primaries, black; tail, black, outer surface showing a tinge of purple; bill and legs, black.
The sexes are similar.
Length 15; wing 10; tail 6; tarsus 1. 75; bill 1.75.

The present species is probably found in different parts of the island, but it is not common. We met with it near the lakes in the vicinity of Gantier, but did not find it elsewhere.

No. Date. Sex. Mus. Locality. Length. Wing. Tail. Tarsus. Bill.
1136 March 6, 1881. 9 C.B.C. j I,1'" 15- 10. 6. 1.75 1.75 1265 March 6, 1881. $ C.B.C. 1iT1"' IS' I0-6' I.7S I.7S FAMILY
TYRANNIDE.
Subfamily, ELAININ/E.
Genus: PITANGUS. Swainsoh.
PITANGUS: SWAINSON, ZOOL. JOURN., III. p. 165, 1828.
PITANGUS GABBII. *Pitangus gabbii.* Lawr., Ann. N. Y. Lye. Nat. Hist., XI. p. 288 (1876). —Cory, Bull. Nutt. Orn. Club, VI. p. 153 (1881). *Sp. Char., Male.* — Top of the head and cheeks, dark brown, the feathers concealing a patch

of bright orange yellow; back, brown, lighter than the head and becoming still lighter towards the rump; wings and tail, brown; the primaries heavily edged with rufous on the outer edge; some of the secondaries showing pale white on the edges; wing coverts and tail-feathers showing rufous edgings; inner webs of primaries and secondaries and some of the under wing coverts edged with yellowish white, giving the under surface of the closed wing a pale yellowish white color; entire under surface, white; b1ll and legs, black.

The sexes are similar.

Length 7.50; wing 4; tail 3.35; tarsus. 85; bill.85.

A resident species, not uncommon in the interior.

XI. p. 90 (1866). — Cory, Bds. Bahama I., p. 99 (1880). — Cory,

Bull. Nutt. Orn. Club, VI. p. 153(1881). *Tyrannus matutinns.* "Vieill., Knc. Meth., p. 850 (1823)." — Gray,

Gen., I. p. 247 (1844). — Salle, P. Z. S., 1857, p. 232. *Tyrannus tiriri.* "Temm., Tabl. Meth., p. 24 (1836)." *Mclittarchus dominicensis.* Cab., J. f. O. , III. p. 478 (1855). — Mus.,

Hein., II. p. 80 (1859). *Lanius tyrannus var. B. dcminicensis.* "Gmel., Syst. Nat., I.

p. 203 (1788)." *Muscicapa dominicensis.* Aud., Orn. Biog., II. p. 392, pi. 46 (1834).

— Bds. Am., I. p. 201, pi. 55 (1840). *Tyrannulus dominicensis.* Jard., Contr. Orn., p. 67 (1850). *Melittarchus griseus.* Gund., Anal, de la Soc. Esp. de Hist. Nat.,

Tomo VII. p. 192 (1878).

Sp. Char., Male. — Above, grayish ash, darkest on the head; a dull black patch behind the eye; underparts, whitish; ashy on the sides of the breast; wings, brown; secondaries and coverts, edged with dull white; under wing coverts, pale yellow; tail, brown; feathers faintly tipped and edged with dull white; upper tail coverts, edged with pale rufous.

The sexes are similar.

Length 8.50; wing 4.40; tail 4.10; tarsus.75; bill.90.

This species is a resident species and very abundant in some localities. The food consists principally of insects of various kinds, which it pursues and catches with great dexterity. A nest taken at Samana, April 18, 1883, contained three eggs which were quite fresh. The eggs have a very pale brownish tinge, heavily blotched with brown and slate color on the larger end. They measure I x yVV inch. The nest is constructed of small twigs loosely put together, and was built in the crotch of a small limb near the ground. Another nest, taken May 20, contained two eggs of much lighter color than the first, and the spotting much finer.

No. Date. Scx. Mus. Locality. Length. Wing. Tail. Tarsus. Bill.
4o5I Nov.12.x882. 9 C. B. C. J, 8.5 4-4 4-'.75-9 Genus: MYIARCHUS. Cabanis.
MYIARCHUS: "CABANIS, FAUX A PERUANA, 1844-46, 152."

MYIARCHUS DOMINCENCIS. *(Biyant.)*
Tyrannula stolida var. dominicencis. Bryant, Proc. Bost. Soc. Nat.

Hist., XI. p. 90 (1866). *Myiarchus ruficandatus.* Cory, Bull. Nutt. Orn. Club, VIII. p. 95 (1883). *Myiarchus stolidus.* Gosse — Cory, Bull. Nutt. Orn. Club, VI.

p. 153 (1881). *Sp. Char., Male.* — Crown, dark olive brown, becoming lighter on the back and showing a more decided grayish tinge; throat and breast, ashy; belly, crissum, and under wing coverts, pale yellow; wing coverts edged with brownish white, forming two dull wing bands; tertials, broadly edged with yellowish white; primaries, except the first, narrowly edged with rufous on the outer rib, showing a broader and much paler edging of the same color on the inner webs of the same feathers; two central tail-feathers, dark brown, all the rest having more than half of the inner web rufous to the tip; bill and feet, black.

The sexes are similar.

Length 6.50; wing 3.10; tail 3; tarsus. 85; bill.75.

This species is generally distributed throughout the island and is common in many localities. A nest taken near Samana, May 5, 1883, contained four eggs of a dull white, blotched at the larger end with slate color and brown. They measure-jn/T x-j6T inch. The nest is a soft structure built of hair, moss, and feathers, and placed in a hole in a tree about four feet from the ground. Incubation had already commenced.

No. Date. Sex. Mus. Locality. Length. Wing. Tail. Tarsus.
3565 Aug.as.188a. 9 C. B. C. s£TM . 6.5 j,,o 3.-85 Genus: CONTOPUS. Cabanis.
CONTOPUS: CABANIS, "JOUJRN. FUR OR. VITfI., III.,.Vav. 1855, 479."

CONTOPUS HISPANIOLENSIS. *(Biyant.)*
Tyrannula carribcea var. hispaniolensis. Bryant, Proc. Host. Soc. Nat. Hist., XI. p. 91 (1866).

Contopus frazeri. Cory, Bull. Nutt. Orn. Club, VIII. p. 94 (1883). *Sayornis dominicensis.* Cory, Bull. Nutt. Orn. Club, VIII. p. 95 (1883). *Sp. Char., Male.* — General plumage, grayish olive; feathers of the crown, dark brown edged with olive; throat ashy, becoming olive on the sides of the breast and yellowish brown on the abdomen and crissum; wing coverts, pale at the tips, forming two very dull wing bands; secondaries, very narrowly edged with pale brownish white; tail, brown; under wing coverts, pale yellowish brown.

The sexes are similar.

Length 5.50; wing 3; tail 2.70; tarsus. 58; bill.52.

In a large collection of skins received from San Domingo, I found two Flycatchers which were unknown to me. They differed so much in size and general appearance that I not only considered them to be distinct species, but placed them in separate genera. The generic differences between a small *Sayornis* and a large *Contopus* are not great, but the difference between the specimens in question was so marked that I had no doubt regarding them until I received a series of thirty-four specimens which intergraded Gknus: EMPIDONAX. Caban.

E.MPIDOXAX: CABANIS, "JOURN. FUR ORNITff., III., Nov. 1855, 480-"

EMPIDONAX NANUS. *Lawr.*
Empidonax nam1s. Lawrence, Ibis, 1875, p. 386.

Sp. Char. — "Above, dull greenish olive, darker on the crown, and brighter on the rump; tail, dark brown, the outer web of the lateral feather pale fulvous; smaller wing coverts the color of the back; the middle and larger coverts are brownish black, ending with white, forming two bars across the wings; the quill-feathers are dark brown, the third and fourth primaries are narrowly edged with grayish white, the inner quills just perceptibly edged with light rufous; under lining of wings, very pale yellow; throat, grayish white; breast, abdomen, and under tail coverts, pale whitish fulvous; thighs, light brown; upper mandible, brown, the under, whitish horn color, dusky on the sides; tarsi and toes, brownish black.

"The first primary is abnormally short, measuring but 1-j5g inches, third quill longest; tail emarginate.

"Length 4f inches; wing 2T; tail 2; bill f; tarsus 8%.

"Hab. St. Domingo; obtained by Prof. W. M. Gabb." *(Lawr., Orig. Deser.)*

Mr. Lawrence remarks: "This appears to be the smallest of the genus yet described. The coloring of the upper plumage is most like that of *E. hammondi;* but it differs in having the breast devoid of ashy coloring, and the abdomen, and especially the under tail coverts, having a decided fulvous tinge; it wants the white margins on the smaller quills, so conspicuous in most of its allies."

The type of the present species has remained unique up to the present time, and it is owing to the courtesy of Mr. Robert Ridgway, who kindly placed it at my disposal, that I have been able to figure it with heads of others of its family.

No. Date. Sex. Mus. Locality. Length. Wing. Tail. Tarsus. Bill.
9SS4I — STM;!" San Domingo. 4.30 2. 12 2.70.37 Genus: ANDROSTOMUS. Gould.

ANDROSTOMUS: *"GOULD, ICONES AL'IUM,* 1838."

ANDROSTOMUS CAROLINENSIS. *(Cm.)*
Caprimulgus carolinensis. Gm., Syst. Nat., I. p. 1028 (1788). — Aud., B. Am. , I. p. 151, pi. 41 (1840). *Antrostomus carolinensis.* Bp., Consp., p. 60 (1850). — Bd., B. N. Am., p. 147 (1858).— Scl., Cat. Am. Bds., p. 280 (1862). — Bd., Bwr. and Ridgw., N. Am. Bds., II. p. 410 (1874). — Gund., Anal, de la Soc. Esp. de Hist. Nat., Tomo VII. p. 201 (1878). — Cory, Bds. Bahama I. , p. 104 (1880). — Cory, Bull. Nutt. Orn. Club, VI. p. 153 (1881). *Caprimulgus brachypterus.* "Steph., Shaw's Gen. Zool., X. p. 150 (1825)?" *Caprimulgus rufus.* Vieill., Ois. Am., Sept. I. p. 57, pi. 25 (9). *Sp. Char., Male.* — Lateral filaments to the bristles of the mouth; general color, pale rufous, mottled with reddish brown; crown streaked with black; feathers of the throat paler, and having the appearance of a brownish bar; terminal two thirds of the tailfeathers, with the exception of the four central ones, rufous white; outer webs, mottled to the tips; quills, mottled and barred with reddish brown.

Female lacking the white on the tail.

Length 11; wing 8; tail 5.50; tarsus. 66; bill,.40.

The present species is probably not uncommon in San Domingo, but on account of its retiring habits is not often seen. Bonaparte describes a species, *A. dominicensis,* from San Domingo, but the two specimens before me do not differ sufficiently to separate them from United States specimens.

No. Date. Sex. Mus. Locality. Length. Wing. Tail. Tarsus. Bill.
1445 Feb. 28, 1881. 9 C.B.C. J L&HP' " 8' 5.5-66.40 *Sp. Char., Afale.* — Above, bark brown variegated with white and tawny; underparts, tawny, banded with brown; throat, tawny, becoming whitish on the breast; a white line from sides of throat to chin; first two primaries with a spot on the inner web, and the second and third with a band of white; edge of carpus, white.

The female differs from the male by having the sides of the throat rufous, instead of white.

Length 8.25; wing 7; tail 4; tarsus.50; bill.20.

This species is abundant in many localities during the summer months.

No. Date. Sex. Mus. Locality. Length. Wing. Tail. Tarsus. Bill 3480 Aug. 4, 1883. J C. B. C. SaDsnago. 8. 25 7-4--SO..o 3485 July 3I, I883. J C. B. C. SaD0. 8.2S 7. 4..5 3468 Aug. 2,,883.

9 C. B. C. soV 8. 7. 4..5 FAMILY CYPSELIDE.

Subfamily, CYPSELINE.
Genus: CYPSELUS. Illig.
CYPSELUS: *ILLIGER, PRODR. SYST. MAMM. ET AVIUM, p.* 229, 1811.
CYPSELUS PHCENICOBIUS. *(Cosse.)*
Tachyornis phoenicobia. Gosse, Bds. Jam., p. 58 (1847). — Gundl., J. f. O., 1856, p. 5.
Cypselus iradii. Lembeye, Aves de Cuba, t. 7, f. 4, p. 50 (1850). *Cypselus phcenicobius.* Scl., P. Z. S., 1865, p. 604. — Cory, Bull.
Nutt. Orn. Club, VI. p. 153 (1881). *Cypselus cayennensis.* Salle, P. Z. S., 1857, p. 232. *Cypselus cayanensis.* Bryant, Pr. Bost. Soc. Nat. Hist., XI. p. 95 (1866).

Sp. Char., Male. — General plumage, dull greenish black; throat, rump, abdomen, and a narrow line in the centre of the belly, white; bill and feet, black. The sexes are similar.

Length 3.75; wing 3.75; tail 1.75; tarsus.20; bill.15.

This little Swift is not uncommon in the interior. At Gantier a large flock were flying about over the town, but they flew very FAMILY TROCHILID:.

Subfamily, POLYTMIN/E, Genus: LAMPORNIS. Swains.
LAMPORNIS: *SWAINSON, ZOOL. JOURX., HI. /.* 358 (1827).
LAMPORNIS DOMINICUS. *(Linn.)*
Trochilus dominicus. Linn., Syst. Nat., p. 191 (1766), 9.— Gmel.,
Syst. Nat., I. p. 489 (1788).
Trochilus margaritaceus. Gmel., Syst. Nat., p. 490 (1788), 9. *Trochilus aurulentus.* Vieill., Ois. Dor., pi. xii. (1802).
— Shaw, Gen.
Zool., VIII. p. 306 (1811).
Lampornis margaritaceus. Bonap., Consp. Gen. Av., I. p. 72 (1850). *Lampornis aurulentus.* "Gould, mon. Trochil., II. pi. 79." — Gund.,
Anal, de la Soc. Esp. de Hist. Nat., Tomo VII. p. 223 (1878).
— Cory, Bull. Nutt. Orn. Club, VI. p. 153 (18S1). *Lampornis virginalis.* "Gould, mon. Trochil., II. pi. 80." *Lampornis dominicus.* Elliot, Ibis, 1872, p. 349. — Elliot, mon.
Trochil., p. 41 (1878).

Lampornis aurulenta. Salle, P. Z. S., 1857, p. 233.

Trochilus (Lampornis) aurulcntus. Bryant, Pr. Bost. Soc. Nat. Hist., XI. p. 95 (1868).

Sp. Char., Male. — Entire upper parts, yellowish green; throat, bright golden green; breast and belly, purplish black; flanks, green, showing a spot of white; under tail coverts, dark purple; wings, purplish brown; outer tail-feathers, violet purple, bordered with steel blue; median feathers, bronze green; bill and feet, black. *Sp. Char., Female.* — Underparts, dull gray, whitening on the throat; tail tipped with white; rest as in the male.

Immature specimens have the underparts dull brownish white, with a line of metallic green passing down the middle of the throat, continuing in a line of black down the middle of the breast and abdomen to the vent.

Length 4.90; wing 2.60; tail 1.85; bill.93.

Very abundant among the mountains at an elevation of one thousand feet and upwards. Although often observed hovering over some flower or perched upon a small twig within a few feet of the ground, it seemed as a rule to prefer the topmost branches of the tallest trees. One huge giant in particular seemed to be an especial favorite. It grew in a small valley upon the outskirts of Petionville, and I rarely passed without observing a dozen or more of this pretty little species darting in and out among its topmost branches, appearing like flies in the distance. It is also common on the coast in the vicinity of Samana.

No. Date. Sex. Mus. Locality. Length. Wing. Tail. Bill.
3325 April c, 1883. $ C. B. C. j,. Sa"lan. a' 1 4.go 2.6o 1.85.93 (ban Domlngo. J 3582 Sept. 3, 1883. C.B.C. sSgo. 4-9 2.60 1.85.90 3959 Dec. 24, 1882. $ C.B. C. j Puerto Plata, j go „ „ (ban Domingo, j' 3952 Dec. 23, 1882. 9 C. B. C. Sa'Jf Domingo, j 4.5 2-S I-6s "9S W&ι, Nov. 16, 1882. 9 C. B. C.-I r. Uer f 4-6o 2.1:0 1.65.ok (San Dom1ngo, j 3944 Dec. 14, 1882. 9 C. B. C. cFue" P?ata 1 4.55 2.5 1.70.95 (San Dom1ngo. j Genus: MELLISUGA. Briss.

MELLISUGA: BRISS., ORXITH., III. p. 695, 1760.

MELLISUGA MINIMA. *(Linn.) Trochilus minimus.* Linn., Syst. Nat., I. p 193 (1766). — Gmel., Syst. Nat., I. p. 500 (1788). — Lath., Ind. Orn., I. p. 320 (1790). *Trochilus minutulus.* Vieill., Ois. Am., Sept. II. p. 73 (1807). *Ornismya minima.* Less., Ois. Mouch., pi. 79 (1829), 9. *Mellisuga humilis.* Gosse, Bds. Jam., p. 127 (1847). *Trochilus catherine.* Salle, Rev. Zool., 1849, p. 498. *Hylocharis niger.* Gray, Gen. Bds. , I. p. 114, sp. 16. *Mellisuga minima.* Bp., Consp. Gen. Av., I. p. 81 (1850). — Gould, mon. Troch., III. pi. 133. — Salle, P. Z. S., 1857, p. 233.— Elliot, Syn. Troch., p. 103 (1878). —Cory, Bull. Nutt. Orn. Club, VI. p. 153 (1881). *Trochilus (Mellisuga) minimus.* Bryant, Pr. Bost. Soc. Nat. Hist., XI. p. 95 (1866). *Sp. Char., Male.* — Above, bright green; flanks, green; throat, dull white spotted with brown, heaviest on the lower part; underparts, white; under tail coverts, tipped with green; tail, black; bill and feet, black. *Sp. Char., Female.* — Resembles the male, but lacks the spots on the throat; lateral tail-feathers, tipped with white.

Length 2.70; wing 1.50; tail.60; bill.45.

Although this little species is abundant in some portions of the island, it is by no means an easy matter to procure specimens. Even after the bird is killed, its extreme smallness and plain coloration render it a difficult object to find amongst the luxuriant tropical vegetation which everywhere covers the ground. I have often observed the male bird perched upon a twig, singing merrily, turning his head from side to side as if greatly enjoying his own music. The song consists of a succession of *tweeps*, often continued for from one to two minutes without intermission, and may be distinctly heard at a distance of thirty yards.

No. Date. Sex. Mus. Locality. Length. Wing. Tail. Bill.
1099 Feb. 17,1881. 9 C.B.C. LeHat"P, 2-7 1.5-6o-45 317S Nov. 24,1882. » C. B.C. sDomSngo. 3'6 ''« '« Genus: SPORADINUS. Reich.

SPORADINUS: REICH., AUFZ. DER COLIB., p. 10, 1853.

SPORADINUS ELEGANS. *Vieitt. Trochilus elegans.* Vieill., Ois. Dor., I. p. 32, pi. xiv. (1802). *Ornismya swainsonii.* "Less., Ois. Mouch., pp. xvii, 197, pi. 70 (1829)." *Lamporris elegans.* Bp., Consp. Gen. Av., I. p. 72 (1850).

Riceordia elegans. Reich., Aufz. der Colib., p. 8 (1853).

Sporadinus elegans. Bp., Rev. and Mag. Zool., 1854, p. 255.—
Gould, mon. Troch., V. pi. 347 (1861). —" Muls., Hist. Nat.
Ois. Mouch., II. p. 72." —Salle, P. Z. S., 1857, p. 233.—
Elliot, Syn. Troch., p. 241 (1878). — Cory, Bull. Nutt. Orn.
Club, VI. p. 153 (1881).

Trochilus (Sporadinus) elegans. Bryant, Pr. Bost. Soc. Nat. Hist.. XI. p. 95 (1866).

Sp. Char., Male. — Upper parts, bronze green; throat, bright metallic green; a portion of the breast, black; wings, brownish purple; tail, dark brown with a bronze lustre on the upper surface; bill, flesh color; tip, black.

Sp. Char., Female. — Above, bronze green; top of head, grayish; underparts, brownish gray; central tail-feathers, bronze green; rest of tail-feathers, gray with subterminal black bar; some of the feathers glossed with green.

Length 4; wing 2.20; tail 1.70; bill.70.

The present species is apparently not common, and very little is known regarding its habits. The measurements are as follows: —

No. Date. Sex. Mus. Locality. Length. Wing. Tail. Kill.
399S April 27, 1883. $ C. B. C. s- 4- . 1.70.70 3580 Sept. 8,1883. $ C.B.C. sJS3goJ 4-2.20,.70.70 3578 Sept. 3,1883. $ C. B. C. j Sa∫TMTM'so j 4— r.7o.70 3579 Sept. 1, r883. 9 C. B. C. g JTM. 4-5 . 1.70.70 3577 Sept 7,.883. 9 C. B. C. ga1f-TM£ga 4.-5-7.70 FAMILY TROGONID:.

Subfamily, TROGONIN.
Genus: TEMNOTROGON. Bonap.

TEMXOTROGOX: "BONAPARTE, CONSP. VOLUCR. ZYGODACT, No. S, p. 14, 1854."

TEMNOTROGON ROSEIGASTER. *Vieitt. Couroucou a ventre rouge, de Saint Dominique.* Buff., Hist. Nat. Ois., VI. p.

287 (1779).
"Le Couroucou a calefon rouge, ou Le Couroucou Damoiscaux.
Le Vaill, Hist. Nat. Cour., pi. 13, p. 18."
Trogon roseigaster. Vieill., Ency. Meth. , III. p. 1358 (1820).—
Gould, mon. Trog., pi. 20 (1838).— Gray, Gen. Bds., I. pt.
1, p. 69 (1849).— Bp., Consp. Av., p. 149 (1850). — Salle,
P. Z. S., 1857, p. 235. —Bryant, Pr. Bost. Soc. Nat. Hist., XI.
p. 95 (1866). *Trogon rhodogaster.* Temm., Nouv. Rec. de Pl. Col. d'Ois. , III. (1820-1839). *Tcmnotrogon roseigaster.* Bp., Consp. Volucr. Zygodact, No. 8, p. 14 (1854). — Gray, Hand List, I. p. 83 (1869). *Temnotrogon rhodogaster.* Scl. and Salv., Nomenc. Av. Neot., p. 103 (1873). *Sp. Char., Male.* — Top of the head, back, and upper tail coverts, lustrous golden green; breast and throat, gray, showing a tinge of green when held in the light; belly and under tail coverts, bright red; primaries and secondaries, dark slaty brown, the outer webs barred with white; wing coverts, green, narrowly barred with white; under surface of tail, dark blue, the three outer feathers having the outer webs and tips white, but showing a spot of black on the outer web near the tip; the inner webs of the two central tail-feathers, dull greenish, extending nearly to the tip, where it is replaced by the blue of the outer web; bill, yellow; feet, brownish,
The sexes are similar.
Length n; wing 5.40; tail 6.40; tarsus. 65; bill.65.
This beautiful species is not very abundant, and seems to be restricted to certain localities. In the mountains back of La Vega it was quite common, and many specimens were taken in the forests which abound in that locality.
No. Date. Sex. Mus. Locality. Length. Wing. Tail. Tarsus. Hiil.
3407 Aug. 9,1883. 9 C.B.C. Sanonngo. "' 5-40 6.40.65.65 3414 Aug. 9,1883. $ C.B.C. SanInfingo. "' S'5 6'2S 65 7 3412 Aug. 9,1883. $ C.B.C. San Dora5- go. j M 5'5 6'2S-6s.7 3403 Aug. 12, 1883. 9 C.B.C. San Domingo. 1I'S S- 4S 6'42 '6s 3404 Aug. 12, 1883. $ C. B.C. SaJDomf ago. n.1o S-48 6.38.66 3408 Aug. 12, 1883. 9 C.B.C. San Donungp. J 10-9S 5'38 6'3 '6s 3405 Aug. 6,1883. 9 C. B. C. sJ;)omfago. " 5-4 6.40.65 3399 Aug. 12, 1883. $ C.B.C. sJaDoSEio. "' 54S 6'3S.6s FAMILY Cuculid:.

Subfamily, S AUROTHERINE, Genus: SAUROTHERA. Vieill.
SAUROTHERA: VIEILLOT, "ANALYSE, *p.* 36, 1816."
SAUROTHERA DOMINICENSIS. *(Lafr.) Saurothera dominicensis.* Lafr., Revue Zool., 1847, p. 355. — Salle, P. Z. S., 1857, p. 234. — Scl., P. Z. S., 1859, p. 378.— Bryant, Pr. Bost. Soc. Nat. Hist. , XI. p. 95 (1866). —Gray, Hand List, II. p. 208 (1870). —Cory, Bull. Nutt. Orn. Club, VI. p. 154 (1881).
Sp. Char., Male. — Head, back, breast, and two central tailfeathers, slate color, darkest on the head, where it sometimes shows a faint brownish tinge, and lightest, being almost ashy, on the breast; wing coverts and tertiaries, slaty gray, showing pale greenish reflections when held in the light; primaries and some of the secondaries, bright rufous brown, the first two edged with dull greenish, and all tipped with the same color; outer tail-feathers, bluish, tipped with white, becoming dull olive at the base; two central tail-feathers tipped with black; throat and abdomen, pale rufous, a bare space encircling the eye, bright red; bill and legs, slaty.
The sexes are similar.
Length 15.50; wing 5.50; tail 9; tarsus 1.40; bill 1.60.
The present species, which is very abundant, is known to the inhabitants as the lizard-catcher, and it is not inappropriately named. It waits quietly, standing perfectly motionless, until a lizard comes within its reach, and then with surprising quickness darts upon and kills it. I have seen lizards four or five inches long killed in this manner. It has a loud, long call, consisting of a series of quickly repeated cries somewhat resembling that of *Colaptes auratus.* The measurements are as follows: —
No. Date. Sex. Mus. Locality. Length. Wing. Tail. Tarsus. Bill.
1255 Feb. 15, 1881. 9 C.B.C. LHaki!P' '5.5 5.5 9-Mo 1-6o
T.... r-T r-f Puerto Plata.) 4145 Jan. 3,1883. g C.B.C. San Domingo, j-'S-SO 5.5 9-1-4 1.60 3716 Jan. 31883. J C.B. C. fisssfe 'S-« 5-48 9-1.40 4.43 Dec. 3o,l882. » C.B.C. ssg. j 1S-aS 5-48 8. 97.40 Dec. 31, 1882. J C.B.C.

Subfamily, CROTOPH AGI Genus: CROTOPHAGA. Linn.
CROTOPHAGA: LINN*f*.US, SYSTAMA NATURE, I. p. 154, 1766.
CROTOPHAGA ANI. *Linn. Crotophaga ani.* Linn., Syst. Nat., I. p. 154 (1766). — Gosse, Bds. Jam., p. 282 (1847).— Bp., Consp., p. 99 (1850). — Salle, P. Z. S., 1857, p. 234. — Scl., P. Z. S., 1860, p. 285; 1861, p. 79. — Scl., Cat. Am. Bds., p. 320 (1862).—Bd., Bds. N. Am. , p. 71 (1858).
— Bryant, Proc. Bost. Soc. Nat. Hist. , XI. p. 95 (1866).— Bd., Bwr. and Ridgw., N. Am. Bds., II. p. 488 (1874). — Gund., Anal, de la Soc. Esp. de Hist. Nat., Tomo VII. p. 233 (1878).
— Cory, Bds. Bahama I., p. 118 (1880).—Cory, Bull. Nutt. Orn. Club, VI. p. 154 (1881).
Crotophaga minor. Less., Traite d'Orn., p. 130 (1831). *Sp. Char., Male.* — Upper mandible much curved, culmen rising above the head, flattened to a sharp edge; nostrils situated in the middle of the lower half of the upper mandible; general color, black, showing bluish reflections; the feathers of the head, neck, breast, and upper part of the back with metallic bronze borders; iris, brown.
The sexes are similar.
Length 12.25; wing 6.20; tail 7.50; tarsus 1.50; bill 1.1o.
An abundant resident species, generally observed in flocks feeding in the fields, or perched upon the branches of some low tree or bush, uttering from time to time a curious but not unmusical whistle. It is not particular as to food; insects, beetles, berries, or fruits being equally acceptable. An egg procured at Jacmel is of a greenish blue color, covered with a white, chalky coating.
No. Date. Sex. Mus. Locality. Length. Wing. Tail. Tarsus. Bill.
4039 Nov.24,1882., C.B.C. «.aS 6.20 7. 50,.5 1.1o *Coceyzus dominicus.* Scl., Cat. Am. Bds., p. 323 (1862).

Cuculus seniculus. Lath., Ind. Orn., I. p. 219 (1790).
Erethroprys seniculus. Bp., List (1838).
Cuculus minor. Bp., Consp. Av., p. 1n (1850).
Sp. Char., Male. — Above, grayish olive, tinged with ash on the head; underparts, yellowish brown, darkest on the thighs, and becoming pale on the throat; a streak of dark brown behind the eye, passing under it; quills and under wing coverts, yellowish brown; outer tail-feathers, black, tipped with white, and showing slight bronze reflections; the others lighter, except the central ones, tipped with white; under mandible, yellow, except at the tip.
The sexes are similar.
Length 11.80; wing 5.20; tail 6.50; tarsus 1.oS; bill.90.
The present species is common and resident; several specimens were taken in different parts of the island.
No. Date. Sex. Mus. Locality. Length. Wing. Tail. Tarsus. Bill.
37is Aug. 7,883. 9 C.B.C. "-80 5- 6.50 j.oS.90 color of the back; primaries with white on the basal half; tail with bands and spots of white. Sp. Char., Female. — Easily distinguished from the male by having the sides of the body and a band across the upper part of the belly light chestnut.
Length 12.50; wing 6; tail 3.65; tarsus. 36; bill 2.
The Kingfisher is a winter visitant, and is often seen about the lakes of the interior. Several specimens were taken.
FAMILY TODID.
Subfamily, TODINE
Genus: TODUS. Linn. *TODUS: BRISSON, t)RN., IV. p. 528, 1760. LINN., SYST. NAT., I. p. 198, 1766.*
TODUS SUBULATUS. ' *Coutd. Le Todier de St. Dominque.* "Buff., Pl. Enl., 585, Figs, 1, 2 (1783)." *Todus viridis.* Vieill. , "N. Diet., XXXIV. p. 184, pi. 29, Fig. 4(1819)." *Todus subulatus.* Gould (Fig. sine, descr.), Gray, and Mitch., Gen. Bds., I. p. 63, pi. 22 (1847). — Bp., Consp., I. p. 182 (1850).
— Gray, Hand List Bds., I. p. 79 (1869). — Sharpe, Ibis, 1874,
P-351*Todus dominicensis.* Lafr., Rev. Zool., 1847, p. 331. — Salle, P. Z.

S., 1857, p. 233. — Bryant, Proc. Bost. Soc. Nat. Hist., XI. p. 91 (1866). — Scl. and Salv., Nom. Avi. Neotr., p. 103 (1873).
— Cory, Bull. Nutt. Orn. Club, VI. p. 154 (1881).
Sp. Char., Male. — Above, bright green; throat, crimson red, the feathers faintly tipped with white; underparts, dull yellowish, the feathers edged with pale red on the basal portions, the color only slightly showing on the surface, and giving the appearance of the chest and belly of being pale yellowish, faintly streaked with red; flanks, pale pinkish red; wings, dark brown edged with green; tail, green; crissum and under tail coverts, pale yellow; a line of dull white extending from the base of the mandible, separating the green of the head from the red of the throat; upper mandible, dark brown; the tip of lower mandible, dull brown.
The sexes are similar.
Length 4.35; wing 2.05; tail 1.60; tarsus.60; bill.70; width of bill at middle. 20.
This peculiar little species is resident and very abundant. They are very pugnacious in disposition, constantly fighting among themselves. Sometimes two would meet in the air, lock their bills together, and whirl round and round until they struck the ground, when, after a short battle, one would fly away, the other following in pursuit. When suddenly surprised it utters a peculiar noise resembling the snort of a pig. A nest taken May 25 was built in a hole in a bank and contained three eggs, which are pure white and measure 170 x Tgoo inch.
No. Date. Sex. Mus. Locality. Length. Wing. Tail. Tarsus. Bill.
39,9 Dec. 1,1882. $ C. B. C. j SaDomingo. 4.3S 2-5 1.6.60.7 3934 March 17, 1882. 9 C. B. C. 1 JaDorMngo. 4.35 2.5 1.6.6 3938 Nov.,8,1882. g C.B.C. nJomSngo. 4.40 2 I.6 '6o 3940 Nov. 24, 1882. $ C.B.C.-I j,,, ',," 4-3 2-1.60 . 60 3927 Dec. 8,1882. $ C.B.C. j Puerto Plata,) 2 6o 6o (San Domlngo, j 39 Nov. 24,,882. 9 C.B.C.-I,,-.. ' 4.40 2. ,,.60.60 (San Domlngo, j " 1074 Feb. ,,88,. $ C.B.C. Portince'j 4.30 2. 1.60.

60 TODUS ANGUSTIROSTRIS. *Lafr. Todus angustirostris.* Lafr., Rev. Zobl., 1851, p. 478. — Salle, P. Z. S., 1857, p. 233. — Bryant, Proc. Bost. Soc. Nat. Hist., XI. p. 91 (1866). — Sharpe, Ibis, 1874, p. 352. Sp. Char., Male. — Above, bright green; throat, dark crimson; the feathers slightly touched with white; underparts, white; flanks, pinkish; under wing and tail coverts, pale yellow; a line of white extending from the base of the mandible, separating the colors of the head and throat, becoming grayish as it reaches the sides of the neck; entire upper mandible and terminal half of lower mandible, dark brown; legs, black.
The sexes are similar.
Length 4; wing 1.90; tail 1.50; tarsus,.45; bill.60; width of bill at middle. 12.
There has been much confusion in regard to the present species, many authors considering it not separable from *T. subulatus.* Salle expresses the belief that *T. angustirostris* is only sexually different from *T. subulatus,* and Dr. Bryant concludes that *angustirostris* is only a narrow-billed specimen of the ordinary San Domingo bird. In the large series now before me are many males and females of both species, and I have unhesitatingly restored the present bird to its rank as a species. Its habits as far as observed appear to be the same as the preceding species.
FAMILY PICIDE.
Subfamily, PICUMNIN.
Genus: PICUMNUS. Temm. *PICUMNUS: TEMMINCK, NOW. REC. DE PL. COL. D'OIS., IV., 1820-1839.*
PICUMNUS LAWRENCEI. *Cory. Chloronerpes passerinus.* Salle, P. Z. S. , 1857, p. 234. *Picus Chloronerpes) passerinus.* Bryant, Pr. Bost. Soc. Nat. Hist., XI. p. 96 (1866). *Picumnus micromegas.* Bryant, Pr. Bost. Soc. Nat. Hist., XI. p. 96 (1866). *Picumnus lawrencei.* Cory, Bull. Nutt. Orn. Club, VI. p. 129 (1881). Sp. Char., Male. — Tail soft, composed of ten feathers; general plumage above, olive green; forehead showing a tinge of black; top of the head, bright yellow, cut by a band of red, again becoming yellow at the

base; underparts, yellowish, palest on the throat, mottled and streaked with brown feathers; on the sides of the neck marked with dull white, nearly joining above, forming an imperfect collar; wing coverts and outer webs of primaries and secondaries, olive green; inner webs, brown, becoming pale on the edges; bill, legs, and feet, dark slate color; iris, reddish brown.

The adult female differs from the male in wanting the red band on the head.

Length 5.10; wing 2.75; tail 1.85; tarsus.70; bill.62.

The present species is abundant in some localities of the interior. It is common near Samana, and several specimens were taken near Le Coup. We generally observed it climbing about the trunks of trees in search of its food. The note is short and sharp, generally uttered while flying. The nest is built in a hole in the trunk of a tree. The eggs were not taken.

forehead and sides of the head, gray; a patch of bright crimson red extending from the forehead to the nape, covering nearly the entire top of the head; rump, crimson red; back alternately banded with black and yellowish green; upper surface of wings having the same appearance of the back, except that they are alternately banded with black and yellow; upper surface of tail, dark brown; bill and feet, dark slate color.

Sp. Char., Female. — Top of head, black; the nape showing bright crimson red, which encroaches slightly upon the black of the head; rest as in the male.

Length 9; wing 4.60; tail 3.60; tarsus. 90; bill 1.20.

This species is very abundant among the mountains. It nests in a hole in the trunk of a tree. The eggs are usually three in number and are pure white. A nest found May 13 contained three eggs which measure 1 X -6$ inch.
k

No. Date. Sex. Mus. Locality. Length. Wing. Tail. Tarsus. Bill.
,-. /- T i-f Puerto Plata,), 4040 Dec. 5,1882. $ C. B.C. gan Domingo' I 9-4-6o 3.60.90 1.20 4042 Dec. 9,,88..? C.li. C. £f£25£. «.8o 4-4 3-60.88
1162 March 9, 1881. $ C. B. C. j Le-j£t"P' 9-4-6o 3.60.90
1128 Feb. 17,1881.? C.B.C. LeH5tJP" 8. 75 4.70 3.75.90
1127 Feb. 18, 1881. S C.B.C. j LeHt"P 8.80 4.40 3.60.90 (.) FAMILY PSITTACID:.

Subfamily, ARIN./E.

Genus: CONURUS. Kuhl.

CONURUS: KUHL, CONS P. PSITT., 4, 1830.,

CONURUS CHLOROPTERUS. *(Souance.)*
Psittacara chloroptera. Souance, Rev. et Mag. de Zool., 1856, p. 59. *Conurus chloropterus.* Scl., P. Z. S., 1857, p. 234. — Finsch, Die Papag. Mon. Bearb., I. p. 469 (1867). *Psittacus (Conurus) chloropterus.* Bryant, Proc. Bost. Soc. Nat. Hist., XI. p. 96 (1866).

Sp. Char., Male. — General plumage, yellowish green, darkest on the tail and wings; under surface of wings and tail, greenish yellow; under wing coverts, bright scarlet, showing upon the edge of the wing; bill, pale; feet, dark brown; some specimens occasionally show feathers tipped with red upon the back and wings, but generally so slightly as to be hardly noticeable. Immature birds often show yellow on the primaries. The sexes are similar.

Length 12; wing 7; tail 6; tarsus.50.

The present species is closely allied to *Conurus pavua*, but may Easily be distinguished from it by numerous constant characters. In *C. pavua* the general color is a darker shade of green. The under surface of the wing is yellow near the red of the carpus, and the entire under surface of quills shows a yellowish tinge. The bird is somewhat larger and the bill is heavier than in *C. chlopterus. C. pavna* has the forehead the same color as the back, while the forehead of *C. chloropterus* shows a yellowish tinge.

The following measurements show the comparative difference in the size of the two species: —

Width of Width of Sex. Length. Wing. Tail. Tarsus. Up. Mand. Low. Mand.
C. pavua $ 13-5 6.95 6..58.60.75 *C. chloropterus* ... $ 12.25 6.75 6..52.5.60

These beautiful birds are not uncommon in some portions of the island. They are gregarious, and frequent the wooded hills of the interior during the winter months. In summer they become much more abundant near the coast.

No. Date. Sex. Mus. Locality. Length. Wing. Tail. Tarsus.
3864 April 7,,883. C. B. C. s'go. » 7-6.. 50 3343 Mar. I2, 1883. 9 C. B. C. Salfgo. ».5« 6.50 6..5 333i April 7,,883. 9 C. B. C. ganSgo .2.5 6.50 6..50 3863 April 9,,883. 9 C. B. C. sTM. ".5 6.5 5.75-48 3340 April 7, 18S3. 9 C. B. C. s J ,,.50 6.5 5.75.5 3733 Sept. 3, 1883. C. B. C. SafS,go. " 6-6'-S

Subfamily, PSITTACIN.

Genus: CHRYSOTIS. Swainson.

CHRYSOTIS: "SWAINSON, ZOOL. JOURN., 1837."

CHRYSOTIS SALLÆI. *Sclater.*

"*Psittacus leucocephalus var.?* Gm., Syst. Nat., I. p. 338." *Chrysotis salhci.* Scl., P. Z. S., 1857, p. 224; Cat. Am. Bds., P-353 (1860). *Psittacus (Chrysotis) sallai.* Bryant, Proc. Bost. Soc. Nat. Hist., XI. p. 96 (1866). *Chrysotis sallei.* Cory, Bull. Nutt. Orn. Club, VI. p. 154 (1881).

Sp. Char., Male. — General plumage, green; forehead, white, extending in front of the eye; top of head, blue, narrowly tipped with black; a patch of black on the cheeks; abdomen and basal half of tail-feathers, crimson, wanting upon the outer web of the outer tail-feather; thighs, pale blue in very adult birds, in most specimens green, the blue being scarcely perceptible; primaries and secondaries, dark blue on the outer webs, inner webs dark brown; a small patch of red on the throat, which does not appear to be constant.

The sexes are apparently similar.

Length 10.50; wing 8; tail 4.50; tarsus.60.

This Parrot is common among the mountains of the interior, and at some localities near the coast; several specimens were seen and one killed at Jeremie, Haiti, and it was abundant at Magua in January.

It is claimed by the inhabitants to be common near Port an Prince during the hot season, but that none are ever seen in winter. FAMILY

No. Date. Sex. Mus. Locality. Length. Wing. Tail. Tarsus.
3364 Jan. 29,,883. *i* C. B. C. SanJHngo. 10.5 8. 4.5-60 3354 Jan.,9,1883. 9 C. B. C. Sa,Sgo. » 7-5 4--60 3360 Mar. 23, I883. 9 C. B. C. sJnDmgo ... 7.5 4--60 36I4 June 1,,883. *S* C. B. C. " "' 7-75 4". 6 3, ngo.

Subfamily, STRIGINE.
Genus: STRIX. Linn.
STXIX: LINX&US, SYST. NAT., I. p. 131, 1766.
STRIX GLAUCOPS. *Kaup. Strix glaucops.* Kaup., "Contr. Orn., p. 118 (1852)"; Id. , Tr. Z. S., IV. p. 246. —Gray, Hand List Bds., I. p. 52. — Pelz., J. f. O., 1872, p. 23. *Strix dominicensis.* Cory, Bull. Nutt. Orn. Club, VIII. p. 95 (1883). *Strix flammed,* Sharpc, Cat. Bds. Brit. Mus., II. p. 292 (1875). *Sp. Char., Male.* — General plumage above, dark brown, shading into orange-rufous on the side of the neck; quills showing inner webs brownish; outer webs, dull orange-rufous, banded with brown; entire underparts, pale orange-rufous, mottled with zigzag marking of light brown, whitening somewhat on the throat and abdomen; face, deep gray; an ante-orbital spot of black; circle of feathers around the face, dark chestnut, bordered with black on the throat; tarsus not feathered to the feet.
Length 13.50; wing 10; tail 4.60; tarsus 2.45.

This form is a somewhat scarce resident. A male was shot Dec. 2, 1882, near Puerto Plata, and another at the same place March 1, 1883. No others were seen, and nothing was learned "-" regarding the habits.

Subfamily, SURNIN/E.
Genus: SPEOTYTO. Gi.oger. *K" SPEOTYTO: GLOGER, HAXDB. NATURG., p.* 226, 1842.
I SPEOTYTO CUNICULARIA. *(Motina) Striv cunicularia.* Molina, Stor. Chil., p. 343 (1782). — Gm., Syst. Nat., I. p. 292 (1788).
Athene cunicularia. Bp., Comp. List Bds. Eur. et N. Am., p. 6.
— Strickl., Orn. Syn., p. 160 (1855). *Speotyto cunicularia var. cunicularia.* Bd., Bwr. and Ridgw., N. Am. Bds., p. 90 (1874).
Speotyto cunicularia dominicensis. Cory, Bull. Nutt. Orn. Club, VI. p. 154 (1881). *Sp. Char., Male.* — General plumage, brown; the head marked with streaks of dull white feathers of the nape showing a subter minal bar of dull white; back, mottled and barred with dusky _ white; quills, brown, tipped With dull white and barred with pale . brown; secondaries marked on the outer web; tail, brown, tipped with buff white, and banded; ear coverts, brown; cheeks, dull white; throat and upper neck, dull white, separated from each other by a mark of sandy buff barred with brownish; underparts, dull white barred with brown, the bars becoming narrower on the lower part of the body; thighs, buff; under wing coverts, yellowish buff, sometimes spotted with brown near the outer edge, and becoming dull white on edge of the wing; tarsus, feathered in front to the foot; iris, yellow.
The sexes are similar.
Length 8; wing 6; tail 2.50; tarsus 1. 50.

Although the same specimens of the San Domingo bird differ somewhat in marking and color from examples taken in other localities, these differences do not seem to be constant. Specimens vary greatly in color which were shot on the same day and in the same locality.

The species is very abundant in the low woods bordering the lakes in the vicinity of Gantier, and we observed it every day during our stay in that locality. A single specimen was taken on the hills back of Port au Prince, but none were observed elsewhere on the island.

No. Date. Sex. Mus. Locality. Length. Wing. Tail. Tarsus.
FAMILY FALCONIDE.
Subfamily, ACC I P IT R I Genus: ACCIPITER. Briss.
ACCIPITER: BRISSON, ORX., I. p. 310, 1760.
ACCIPITER FRINGILLOIDES. *Vigors. Accipiter fringilloidcs.* Vig., "Zool. Journ. , III. p. 434 (1828)." — Scl. and Salv. , Nom. Av. Neotr., p. 120 (1873). — Sharpe, Cat. Bds. Brit. Mus., I. p. 135 (1874).
Nisus fringilloides. D'Orbigny, "Ramon de la Sagra, N. H. Cuba Ois., p. 18 (1839)." *Nisus fuscus.* Cory, Bull. Nutt. Orn. Club, VI. p. 154 (1881). *Sp. Char., Female.* — Resembles *Aceipiter fuscus,* but plumage much paler; above, brown, the concealed portions of the feathers showing much white; concealed feathers of the back regularly marked with broad spots of white; tail, pale brown, showing five somewhat indistinct bands of darker brown; under surface of tail, dull white, regularly banded with brown; breast and belly, white, the shafts of 'the feathers dark brown, showing hair-like lines over the whole surface: these lines are in many cases bordered with pale brown, giving the appearance of arrow-shaped markings; under tail coverts, white; quills, brown, barred with white on the inner webs; under surface of wings, white, barred with brown.
Length 11.50; wing 7; tail 5.50; tarsus 1.75.

A single specimen of this interesting form was killed near Le Coup in March. No others were seen.

No. Date. Sex. Mus. Locality. Length. Wing. Tail. Tarsus.
1276 March3,1881. 9 C. B. C. J LeH£"P' .".5 7-5.5 '-75 Genus: RUPORNIS. Kaup.
RUPORNlS: KAUP, CLASSIF. SAUG. U. VOG., 1844.
RUPORNIS RIDGWAYI. *Cory. Rnpornis ridgwayi.* Cory, Journ. Bost. Zool. Soc. , II. p. 46 (1883); Auk, I. p. 4 (1884). *Sp. Char., Male.* — Above, slaty brown; shafts of the feathers of the head and upper back, dark brown; underparts, slaty, faintly touched with rufous on the belly and abdomen; chin, dull white; shoulders and thighs, rufous, the latter much the brighter, and faintly pencilled with indistinct pale lines; wings and tail, dark brown, imperfectly banded with dull white, and showing various shadings of a rufous tinge; all.the outer primaries imperfectly banded with white, gradually becoming fainter on the outer webs, until just perceptible on the sixth, the rest of primaries and secondaries, with the outer web, dark brown; and the inner webs thickly banded with white,

showing traces of rufous.
Length 13.75; wing 9.15; tail 6; tarsus 2.75; bill 1.20.
S/. Clutr., Female. — Top of the head and neck, brownish ash, becoming darker on the back; the feathers of the back and tertiaries edged with rufous; underparts, dark rufous, the feathers narrowly banded with white; thighs showing the rufous much brighter, the feathers banded with very fine pale lines; crissum, white, with rufous bands near the tips; underpart of breast, slaty, shading into dull white on the throat; the shafts of the feathers on the throat and breast dark brown, showing in hair-like lines; the rest as in the male.
Length 14.50; wing 10; tail 6.45; tarsus 2.65; bill 1.25.
Immature Male. — In general appearance much like *Buteo pcnnsyfoanicus;* underparts, dull white, the feathers slightly tinged with rufous, the centre of the surface feathers showing a stripe of brown, giving the body a striped appearance; thighs, rufous, but paler than in the adult; above, much resembling the adult; the white wing and tail bands replaced by rufous bands on the terminal half of the feathers.
This species seems to be not uncommon in the valley of the Yuma River, but it is nowhere abundant. Nothing is known regarding its habits.
No. D.ltc. Sex. Mus. Locality. Length. Wing. Tail. Tarsus.
3364 Jan. 31, 1883. 9 C. B. C. j c M:Jsua' j 14.50 10. 6.45 2.65 (San Domlngo, j 326, April 3,.883. 9 C.B.C. SalfD';TM0. 14-lo. 6. 2.6o 54,0 Sept. 4. .883. C. B. C. jjTM I3.a5 9-40 6. 2.6o 3419 Aug. 27,,883.? C. B. C. SaTMo 13. 75 9-'S 6. 2.65
Subfamily, FALCONIN/E.
Genus: FALCO. Linn.
FALCO: LIXXSEUS, SYST. NAT., I. p. 124, 1766.
FALCO COLUMBARIUS. Linn. *Falco columbarius.* Linn., Syst. Nat., I. p. 128 (1766). — Gm., Syst.
Nat., p. 281 (1789).— Daud., Tr. Orn., II. p. 83 (1800).—
Shaw, Zool., VII. p. 188 (1812). — Wils., Am. Orn., pi. xv. f. 3 (1808). — Gosse, Bds. Jam., p. 17

(18471. — Sagra, Hist.
Nat. Cuba Ois., p. 23. — Cory, Nat. Magdalene I., p. 56 (1878).
— Coucs, Key N. Am. Bds., p. 536 (1884).
Tinmtnculus columbarius. Vieill., Ois. Am., Sept., I. pi. xi. (1807). *Hypotriorchis columbarius.* Gray, List Bds. Brit. Mus., p. 55 (1844). — Gen. B., fol. sp. n (1844). — Cass., Bds. Cal. and Tex., p. 90 (1854). — Gundl., Anal. Soc. Esp. Hist. Nat., Tomo VII. p. 162 (1878).
Lithofalco columbarius. Bp., Consp. Av., p. 26 (1850). *sEsalou columbarius.* Kaup., Mon. Falc. Cont. Orn., p. 54 (1850). *Sp. Char., Male.* — Above, umber brown; feathers of the head with distinctly showing black shafts; tail, brown, banded and tipped with dull white; underparts, dull white, longitudinally streaked with brown, the blotching heaviest on the breast; throat, generally immaculate; flanks, barred and spotted; a slight superciliary streak; iris, brown; feet and legs, yellow; bill, bluish black; cere and base of the bill, yellowish green. Very old males have 'the upper parts slaty blue, but specimens are rarely met with. The female resembles the immature male, as above described. coverts, bluish; tail-feathers, with the exception of the central ones, bluish, with a black band about an inch from the tip; a slight streak of metallic blue below the ear; quills, dark brown; secondaries, tipped with white; feet, red.
Length 11; wing 7.50; tail 5; tarsus 1. 20.
A single specimen of this Hawk was killed at Puerto Plata. Its measurements are as follows: —
No. Date. Sex. Mus. Locality. Length. Wing. Tail. Tarsus.
447 Ic.,,,881. $ C.B.C n. 7.5 5-1.20 FALCO SPARVERIUS ISABELLINUS (L.). Swain. Faho isabcllinus. Swain., An. Mcnag., p. 281 (183.8). *Tinnunculus sparverins var. isabellim1s.* Ridg., P. A. N. S. Phila.,
Dec., p. 149 (1870); Bd., Bwr. and Ridgw., N. Am. Bds., III.
p. 171 (1874). *Tinnunculus dominiccusis* "(not of Gmel.. Strickl., Orn. Syn. , I. ioo (1855)." *Faleo domiuicensis.*

Bryant, Proc. Bost. Soc. Nat. Hist., XI. p. 90 (1866). *Tinmtnculus sparverius var.?* Cory, Bull. Nutt. Orn. Club, VI. p. 154 (1881). *Sp. Char., Male.* — Top of head, slate color; forehead, whitish; throat, white; a maxillary and auricular black stripe; breast, rufous; back, dark rufous brown; tail, rufous brown, tipped with white, and having a subtcrminal band of black; outer web of outer tail-feather, white; wing coverts, slate color; abdomen and belly, white; a patch of black on the side of the neck. *S/. Char. , Female.* — Top of head, slate color, showing a patch of rufous; entire upper parts, rufous brown, banded with dull black; underparts, very pale rufous, delicately streaked and spotted with brown; throat, white.
Length 10; wing 7; tail 5; tarsus 1.20.
This Sparrow Hawk is not uncommon in San Domingo. All the specimens taken varied but little in coloration.
No. Date. Sex. Mus. Locality. Length. Wing. Tail. Tarsus.
3Iso Dec. 24,,88,. 9 C.B.C. 1--.,a 7-5-4428 Dec. S,,883. *t* C.B.C. £2£.-? 5.35-o 3279 Jan. 7,1883. $ C.RC gjgcj.a *j.* 5-5 i.«o 3I49 Dec. 25,1882. 9 C. B. C. j cPuerA P!ata' 1 10.50 8. 5.25 (San Domlngo, j 1.20 *Falco americanus.* "Gm., Syst. Nat., p. 257 (1788)." — "Shaw,
Zool., VII. p. 88." *Aquila americana.* Vieill., Ois. Am., Sept., I. pi. iv. (1807). *Paudion americanus.* Vieill., Gal. Ois., pi. ii. (1825). — Vig., Zobl.
Journ., I. p. 336.
Acelpiter piscatorius. Catesby, Carolina, I. pi. ii. (1754).
Pandion haluctus. Rich., Faun. Bor. Am., II. p. 20(1831). — Aud., Orn. Biog., I. p. 415 (1831). — Gray, List Bds. Brit. Mus., p. 22 (1844). — Cory, Bds. Bahama I., p. 131 (1880). — Coues,
Key N. Am. Bds., p. 556 (1884).
Sp. Char., Male. — Above, dark brown; head, white, somewhat marked with dark brown on crown and cheeks, varying in specimens; underparts, white, sometimes streaked with light brown, especially on the breast; feet, very large, bluish.

Length 22; wing 18.50; tail 9; tarsus 2.40; bill 1.40.

The species is probably a winter visitant in San Domingo; no specimens were taken, but one was seen at Port an Prince. It is found in Cuba, and is common in the Bahama Islands.

& tail-feathers like the back, the others dark brown; two outer feathers tipped with white; upper surface of wing showing large spots of bluish purple; bill and feet, yellowish, the former becoming dark at the tip.

Length 6.30; wing 3.30; tail 2.60; tarsus.50; bill.50.

This graceful little Dove is a resident and abundant. Incubation commences in May. The nest is loosely constructed, and made of grass and small sticks. The eggs are generally two in number and pure white.

Length 10; wing 6; tail 4.50; tarsus. 80; bill.55.

This handsome Dove is resident in San Domingo, but is seldom seen, owing to its solitary disposition. Incubation commences in May. A nest of this species, taken in the Bahama Islands, was composed of loose sticks placed in the crotch of a fallen tree about three feet from the ground, and contained two white eggs. Dr. Bryant, who found it breeding in the Bahamas, states that all nests found by him were placed in holes in the rocks.

No. Date. Sex. Mus. Locality. Length. Wing. Tail. Tarsus.
4426 Jan. 4, 1883. i C. B. C. gJJ. '« 6. 4.5-80 3"9 Feb''''883. C. B. C. SanMDsgo. ' 4.5-80 3292 Feb. I1883. C. B. C. sJsgo. " «« W 3,90 Feb. Ifl883. 9 C.B.C. 9.75 5-9 4.5-So *Eclopistes caroliucnsis.* — Rich., List, 1837.— Bp. , List, p. 41 (1838). *Zcnaidura caroliucnsis.* "Bp., Consp., II. p. 84 (1854)." — Scl., P. Z. S., 1856, p. 359. —Salle, P. Z. S., 1857, p. 235.—Bcl., Bds. N. Am., p. 604 (1858).— Lawr., Ann. Lyc. , IX. p. 139; IX. p. 207.— Bd., Bwr. and Ridgw., N. Am. Bds., III. p. 383 (1874).—Cory, Bull. Nutt. Orn. Club, VI. p. 154 (1881).— Cones, Key N. Am. Bds., p. 568 (1884). *Columba marginata.* Linn., Syst. Nat., I. p. 286 (1766).

— Gm., Syst. Nat., I. p. 791 (1788). *Sp. Char., Alale.* — Above, including middle tail-feathers, pale bluish gray, shaded with brownish; head and neck brownish, tinged with dull blue; sides of the neck showing golden and red iridescence; a purplish black spot under the ear coverts; underparts. pale purplish, becoming ochraceous on the belly and crissum; chin, dull white; quills, dull slate color; tail-feathers, slate color, the outer eight tipped with white; bill, black; bare skin around the eye, bluish; feet, red; iris, brown.

Length 10.25; wing 5.75; tail 5; tarsus. 60.

A single bird of this species was shot near Le Coup on March 1. It was Hying across an open field in company with another, probably the female; no others were seen, and we did not meet with it afterwards.

No. Date. Sex. Mus. Locality. Ixngth. Wing. Tail. Tarsus.
1249 March 1, 1881. i C. B. C. LJ"P' 10. 25 5.75 5--6 Genus: MELOPELIA. Bonap. *MELOPELIA: BOXAP., CONSP., II. p.* 81, *1854.*

MELOPELIA LEUCOPTERA. *(Linn.) Columba leucoptera.* Linn., Syst. Nat., I. p. 164 (1758). — Gm., Syst. Nat., I. p. 773 (1788). *Zcnaida leucoptera.* "Gray, Gen. Bds." *Turtur leucopterus.* Goss-e, Bds. Jam., p. 304 (1847). *Melopelia Icucoptera.* Bp., Consp. Av., II. p. 81 (1854). — Bd., Bds.

N. Am., p. 603 (1858). — Coop., Orn. Cal., I. p. 515 (1870).—

Bd., Bvr. and Ridgw., N. Am. Bds. , III. p. 376 (1874). — Coues, Key N. Am. Bds., p. 569 (1884).

"*Colnmba trudcaui.* And., Bds. Am., VII. p. 352 (1843)."

Sp. Char., Male. — General color, ashy, showing an olive tinge on the upper surface; primaries and secondaries, brownish black; beneath, pale ash; sides and abdomen showing a bluish tinge; lower portion of abdomen, white; a tinge of purple ori the occiput; a spot of steel blue-black under the ears; a large patch of white on the wings, extending over the lower coverts from the carpus to the secondaries; a faint golden purple reflection on the neck and throat. The female is similar to the male, but lacks the tinge of golden on the throat, which shows but slightly, if at all.

Length 11.25; wing 6.25; tail 4.25; tarsus.80.

A single specimen of this species was taken at Puerto Plata in January. The measurements are as follows: —

No. Date. Sex. Mus. Locality. Length. Wing. Tail. Tarsus.
/-i /- f Puerto Plata,), 4425 Jan. 2,1883. 3 C.B.C. San Domi;go'. j 11.25 6.25 4.25-80 Gknvs: GEOTRYGOX. Gosse. *GKOTRYGOX: GOSSE, liDS. JAM., p.* 316, 1847.

GEOTRYGON MONTANA. *(Linn.) Columba montana.* Linn., Syst. Nat., I. p. 281 (1766).— Gm., Syst.

Nat., I. p. 772 (1788 — Wagl., Syst. Av., 1827, p. 75. *Perist'era montana.* Gray, Gen. Bds., II. p. 475. *Geotrygon moutana.* Gosse, Bds. Jam., p. 320 (1847). — Cab.,

Journ., IV. p. 109 (1856). — Salle, P. Z. S., 1857, p. 235.—

March, Bds., p. 300 (1863).— Gundl. , Anal. Soc. Esp. Hist.

Nat., Tomo VII. p. 348 (1878). *Columba (Gcotrygou) moutana.* Bryant, Proc. Bust. Soc. Nat. Hist., XI. p. 96 (1866).

Sp. Char., Alale. — Above, purplish brown, becoming light brown on the wings; throat, dull white, becoming pale purple on the breast; belly, pale brown, becoming brownish white on the under tail coverts. *Sp. Char., Female.* — Upper parts, greenish brown; forehead, light brown, the color extending upon the cheeks and sides of the head; breast, chestnut brown.

Length 9.25; wing 6; tail 3.25; tarsus I.

A very abundant resident species, generally to be met with in flocks frequenting large growth. The measurements are as follows: — GEOTRYGON MARTINICA. *(Cm) Columba martinica.* Gm., Syst. Nat., I. p. 781 (1788).

Geotrygon martinica. Bp., Consp. Av., II. p. 74 (1854). — Gundl.,

Anal. Soc. Esp. Hist. Nat., Tomo VII. p. 347 (1878). — Cory,

Bds. Bahama I., p. 141 (1sso). — Coues, Key N. Am. Bds., p. 57I (1884).

Orcopeleia martinicana. Reich., Syst. Av., p. 25 (1851).
Orcopcleia martinica. Bd., Bds. N. Am. , p. 607 (1858). — Gundl., Repert. Cub., I. p. 299 (1866). — Bd., Bwr. and Ridgw., N. Am. Bds., III. p. 393 (1874). *Columba (Geotrygoli) martinica.* Bryant, Proc. Bost. Soc. Nat. Hist., XI. p. 96 (1866).

Sp. Char., Male. — Above, chestnut-rufous; crown and neck with metallic reflections of green and purple; back showing brilliant purple reflections, becoming less distinct on the rump; a band of white from the base of the lower mandible under the eye to the side of the neck, bordered below by a streak of dull purple; underparts showing the breast pale purple, becoming dull white on the throat and abdomen; primaries, bright rufous, becoming darker at the tips; tail, rufous; legs, light red; bill, red; lip, horn color; iris, light brown. XI. p. 96 (1866). —Bd., Bwr. and Ridgw., N. Am. Bds., III.

Length 10.75; wing 6; tail 4.25; tarsus 1.05; bill.90.

This beautiful Pigeon is resident, and probably not uncommon, although on account of its preference for the heavily wooded portions of the island it is not as often met with as the other species. The note is low and mournful, and is heard during the early hours of morning.

No. Date. Sex. Mus. Locality. Length. Wing. Tail. Tarsus.
5.34 Dec.18,1882. S C.B.C. 10.75 6. 4-5-5 p. 363 (1874).— Cory, Bds. Bahama I., p. 137 (18So).—
Cory, Bull. Nutt. Orn. Club, VI. p. 154 (1ss1). — Coues, Key
N. Am. Bds., p. 565 (1884). *Patagicenas leucocephalus.* Reich., Syst. Av., XXV. (1851).— Bp.,
Consp., II. p. 54 (1854). —" Gundl., Cab. Journ., 1856, p. 107." *Patagicenas leucocephala.* Gundl., Anal. Soc. Esp. Hist. Nat., Tomo VII. p. 345 (1878).

Sp. Char., Male. — Above, grayish blue, showing slight reflections; crown, pure white, bordered at the nape by a band of dark purple, and below it a cape extending upon each side of the neck of metallic green, showing blue in some lights, the feathers bordered with black; quills, dark brown, becoming lighter upon the secondaries; underparts, grayish blue; crissum, plumbeous; tail, very dark brown.

The female resembles the male, but is somewhat paler.

Length 12.50; wing 7.25; tail 5.25; tarsus.80.

A resident species, very abundant in the interior. The natives claim that during the summer they are gregarious, and are found in immense flocks in some localities. Incubation commences in May.

No. Date Sex. Mus. Locality. Length. Wing. Tail. Tarsus.
3876 Jan. 3-883. 3 C.B.C. sP;X±go. 12'5 7-S 5-5-So 4r.8 Dec. a9,,88a. 9 C JJJJJ .3. 7-5 5-5-So 3886 De,2I,l88, 9 C. B. C. *jff* » 8. 5..8 COLUMBA INORNATA. rigors. *Columba inornata.* Vigors, P. Z. S., 1847, p. 37.— De la Sagra,
Voy. i'Ile de Cuba Ois., Tomo XXVIII. —Cab. Journ., IV.
p. 106 (1856). —Scl., P. Z. S., 1861, p. 80; March, P. A. N. S.,
1863, p. 301. —Gulld!., Repert. Cub., I. p. 298 (1866). —Bd.,
Bwr. and Ridgw., N. Am. Bds., III. p. 360 (1874).
Columba ruflua. "Gosse, Bds. Jam., p. 296 (1847)."
Chlorcenas inornata. Gundl., Anal. Soc. Ksp. Hist. Nat., Tomo VII. p. 343 (1878).

Sp. Char., Male. — Head, neck, underparts, and some of the wing coverts, dull purple; rest of plumage, slaty; edges of outer webs of some of the wing coverts, white, distinctly marking thewing; chin, dull white.

The sexes are similar.

Length 14.50; wing 8.50; tail 5.50; tarsus 1.1o.

This species was observed only upon one occasion, at Magua, where a single specimen was shot. The following are the measurements: —

No. Date. Sex. Mus. Locality. Length. Wing. Tail. Tarsus.
3259 Feb. 2, ,883. S C.B.C. Sal;Slgo. '4.5 8'5 5.5...o p. 108.—Bryant, Proc. Bost. Soc. Nat. Hist., XI. p. 96 (1866). — lid., But. and Ridgw., N. Am. Bds., III. p. 360 (1874). *Patagiffnas corensis.*
Gundl., Anal. Soc. Esp. Hist. Nat., Tomo VII. p. 344 (1878). *Sp. Char., Male.*
— General plumage, slaty; top of head, throat, and breast, pale purple; a broad cape extending from the sides of the neck, over the upper back, of beautifully rounded feathers, showing bright metallic purple when held in the light, each feather narrowly edged with dark brown at the base of the skull.

The sexes are similar, the female being slightly paler.

Length 13.50; wing 7.50; tail 5.50; tarsus 1.

Two specimens of this interesting bird were taken near Magua; none were observed elsewhere. Their measurements are as follows: —

No. Date. Sex. Mu.?. Locality. Length. Wing. Tail. Tarsus.
3-5r Tan. 29,1883. $ C. B. C. *c* Magua, J 3 j San Domlngo, j J 3
Jan. 27, 1883. 9 C.B.C. c n£,', 14-8.50 5.75 *Sfi. Char., Male.* — Above, rich brownish red, mottled with black; crown, black, shading into brown at the base of the skull, and mottled with black and white on the nape; a white superciliary line passing from nostril to nape; throat, white, bordered broadly with black; upper breast and sides, reddish brown, shading into white on the belly, the feathers thickly banded with black; crissum, reddish brown; tertials and some of the wing coverts, edged with yellowish white; bill, entirely black.

Sp. Char., Female. — Resembles the male; the white of the head and throat replaced by tawny, without black edging.

Length 8.50; wing 4.50; tail 2.50; tarsus 1; bill.52.

The Partridge was introduced many years ago, according to the statement of the inhabitants. At the present time it is not uncommon, but is very difficult to procure, on account of the almost impenetrable thickets which abound in the localities which it frequents. The specimens taken approach very closely in coloration to the Bahama form, but are lighter and much less black on the breast than that which is found in Florida.

FAMILY

CHARADRIID/E

Subfamily, CEDICN EM INE,

Genus: GEDICNKMUS. Tk.mm. (7-:DIC,V£.llt'S: TKM.II., M.IA'. D'ORX., 1815.

CEDICNEMUS DOMINICENSIS. *Cory. (Edicnemus dominicensis,* Cory, Journ. Zuol. Soc., II. p. 46 (1883); Auk, I. p. 4 (1884). *Sp. Char., Male.* — Top of the he.id, back, wing coverts, and tail, brown; feathers with very pale edgings, giving a mottled appearance to the back; the tail-feathers showing a band of dull white, succeeded by a broad black tip; breast, slaty, becoming dull white on the throat; abdomen, white, tinged with very pale rufous; a line of black passing from the top of the eye along the sides of the head to the neck; under surface of wings, white, becoming dark brown at the tips; the shafts of the feathers on the breast and throat, dark brown, forming numerous hair-like lines on the surface of the plumage; legs and feet, greenish yellow; upper mandible, black; under mandible, green at the base, shading into black at the tip; iris, yellow.

The sexes appear to be similar.

Length 14.50; wing 8.50; tail 3.75; tarsus 3.75; bill 1.50.

The present species seems to be restricted to the eastern portion of the island, as none were met with elsewhere. It is not uncommon on the high hills back of La Vega. Mr. M. A. Frazer, in a letter regarding this species, says, "Although I found it feeding during the day, it seems somewhat nocturnal in. its habits, as I saw them in comparative abundance in a large savanna, through which I passed at midnight on my return from La Vega.... Their note is a repetition of the syllable 'tu,' repeated very rapidly." lie also says that the natives tame the birds and keep them in the houses for the purpose of killing the spiders and bugs which abound in large numbers, and which it greedily kills and eats. It is known to the inhabitants by the name of Boukera.

No. Date. Sex. Mus. Locality. Length. Wing. Tail. Tarsus.

sEgialitis vociferus. Bp., Comp. List, p. 45 (1838). — Gosse, Bds. Jam., p. 330 (1847). —Salle, P. Z. S., 1857, p. 236.— Cory, Bds. Bahama I., p. 145 (1880). — Coues, Key N. Am. Bds., p. 600 (1884). *Oxyechus vociferus.* Reich., Syst. Av., 1853, pi. xviii. — Gundl., Anal. Soc. Esp. Hist. Nat., Tomo VII. p. 382 (1878).— Ridg., Nom. N. Am. Bds., No. 516 (1881). —Bd., Bwr. and Ridgw., N. Am. V Bds., I. p. 148 (1884). *Charadrius torquatus.* Linn., Syst. Nat., I. p. 225 (1766). *Charadrius jamaicensis.* Gm., Syst. Nat., I. p. 685 (1788). *Charadrius (/Egialitis) vociferus.* Bryant, Proc. Bost. Soc. Nat. Hist., XI. p. 97 (1866).

Sp. Char., Jlfalc. — Above, dark olive brown; throat, white, continuing in a band around the neck, edged below with black; narrow upon the back, and broad upon the upper part of the breast, the black band of the breast again succeeded by one of white, shading into the color of the back upon the sides, and that, in turn, by still another band of black, reachinr to the wines, the *J O O'* feathers of the latter edged with white; forehead, white, the band touching the eyes and succeeded by a black bar across the crown;

O *j* a superciliary line of tawny white reaching nearly to the nape; underparts, white; rump, orange brown; tail-feathers, except the central, white (at tips), orange, and black in turn, becoming white again at the base; primaries edged and, except the first two, tipped with white; secondaries and coverts tipped with white, forming a bar. Length 10; wing 6.50; tail 3.80; tarsus 1.50; bill.80.

Dr. Bryant found this species in San Domingo, and it is recorded from Cuba and Porto Rico. It was not met with by our party.

GIALITIS WILSONIUS. Ord. *Charadrius wilsonius.* "Ord., ed. Wils., IX. p. 77 (1825)." — Nutt., Man. Orn., II. p. 21 (1834). — Aud., Orn. Biog., III. p. 73 (1835). *&gialites wilsonius.* Bp., Consp. List, p. 45 (1838). — Coues, Check List, 2d ed., No. 585 (1882). *sEgialitis wilsonius.* Cass., in Bds. B. N. Am., p. 693 (1858).—

Bel, Cat. N. Am. Bds., No. 506 (1859.) —Coues, Key N. Am. Bds., p. 244 (1872).— Cory, Bds. Bahama I., p. 147 (1881).—

Coues, Key N. Am. Bds., p. 601 (1884). *Ochthodromus wilsonius.* Reich., Syst. Av., XVIII. (1853).— Gundl., Anal. Soc. Esp. Hist. Nat., Tomo VII. p. 381 (1878).—Bd., But. and Ridgv., N. Am. W. Bds., I. p. 168 (1884).

Sp. Char., Male. — Above, ashy brown; forehead, white, extending into a faint superciliary stripe of dull black on the crown; throat white, continuing on the sides of the neck, nearly joining upon the nape; a black pectoral band, the feathers edged with white, becoming brown upon the sides; underparts, white; two central tail-feathers, brown, the others showing increasing markings of white to the outer tail-feathers, which are white; bill, black (large and stout); legs, pinkish.

Female and immature birds have the pectoral band brown, and no black on the head.

Length 7.45; wing 4.60; tail 1.90; tarsus 1.16; bill.90.

A specimen in my collection is labelled Port au Prince, Haiti. It has been taken in Cuba, and Gundlach records it from Porto Rico. None were observed by our party.

. *Char., Male.* — Bill short and stout, of an orange-yellow ipped with black; legs, yellowish; toes, semipalmate; above, grayish brown, with coronal and pectoral bars of dark brown; ds, orange. Length 6.75; wing 4.50; tail 2.35; tarsus.80; bill.40. color, tipped with black; legs, yellowish; toes, semipalmate; above, . eyelids, orange.

This Plover is a winter visitant, and apparently not common. A single specimen was taken at Puerto Plata in December.

FAMILY ILEMATOPHODnXE.

Subfamily, HEMATOPHODIN/E.

Genus: HMATOPHUS. Linn.

HsEMATOPUS: LI.V., SYST. NAT, Ed. 10, /. 152 (1758); *Ed.* 12, /. 257 (1766).

H/EMATOPUS PALLIATUS. *Tcmm. Heematopus palliatus.* Tcnm., Man., II. p. 532 (1820). — And., Orn. Biog., III. p. 181 (1835).—Bd., Bds. N. Am., p.

699 (1858). — Coues, Key N. Am. Bds. , p. 246 (1872). — Gundl., Anal. Soc. Esp. Hist. Nat., Tomo VII. p. 379 (1878). — Cory, Bds. Bahama I., p. 150 (1880). — Ridg., Nom. N. Am. Bds. , No.'507 (1881).—Bd., Bwr. and Ridgw., N. Am. W. Bds., I. p. 112 (1884). — Cones, Key N. Am. Bds., p. 606 (1884). *H&matopus arcticus.* "Jard. , ed. Wils., III. p. 35 (1832)." *"Hcematopus ostralegus.* Wils., Am. Orn., VIII. p. 15, pi. Ixiv. (1814)." *Sp. Char.,.Male.* — Head and neck, blackish or very dark brown; back, brown; lower part of breast and rest of underparts, white; eyelids, rump, tips of wing coverts, part of secondaries, and . basal portion of the tail-feathers, white; bill, orange, darkening at the tip (in summer deep red); legs, flesh color.

Length 17.40; wing 10.05; tail 4-35! tarsus 2.30; bill 3.50.

The present species probably occasionally visits San Domingo. None were observed by our party, but the inhabitants described it, stating that it was not uncommon. pink; bill, black; iris, orange. Immature birds have the upper plumage brownish. with white and brown; throat, ashy, shading into olive on the sides of the breast; a faint superciliary line of dull white touching the eyelid; abdomen and crissum, white; secondaries tipped, and inner primaries spotted with white; lower mandible, greenish, becoming dark at the end.

Length 13.50; wing 8; tail 2.70; tarsus 4.20; bill 2.75.

Dr. Bryant records this species from San Domingo; and although I did not meet with it, the inhabitants informed me that it was common in some localities.

Length 7.10; wing 3.75; tail 2.05; tarsus.94; bill 1.

The spotted Sandpiper is probably a rather scarce winter visitant. Two specimens were taken near Port au Prince in February, and three at Jacmel, during the latter part of March.

The following species, although not recorded from San Domingo, undoubtedly occur there during the migrations. Most of them are common in Cuba, and Gundlach records them all in his list of the birds of Porto Rico: *Ereunetes pusillus, Ercnnctcs minutilla, Tringa maculata, Calidris arenaria, Liwosa-fcdoa, Totalms semipalmatus, Tolanus mclanoleucus, Totanus flavipes, Totanus solitarius, Numenius hudsonicus,* and *Numcnius borcalis.* FAMILY TANTALID.

Subfamily, EUDOCIMIN/E.
Genus: EUDOCIMUS. Wagler.
EUDOCIMUS: WAGLER, 7.V/.9, 1832, /. 1232.

EUDOCIMUS ALBUS. *(Linn.) Scolopax alba.* — Linn., Syst. Nat., I. ed. 10, p. 145 (1758). *Tantalus alber.* Linn., Syst. Nat., I. p. 242 (1766). *Tantalus albus.* Gm., Syst. Nat., I. p. 651 (1788). — Wils., Am.

Orn., VIII. p. 43, pi. 66 (1814). *Ibis alba.* Yicill., Nouv. Diet, XVI. p. 16 (1817).— Nutt., Man.

Orn., II. p. 86 (1834). — And., Eds. Am., VI. p. 54, pi. 360 (1843)*Eudocimus albus.* Wagl., Isis, 1832, p. 1232. — Gundl., Anal. Soc.

Esp. Hist. Nat., Tomo VII. p. 364 (1878). — Ridg., Nom. N. Am. Bds., No. 501 (1SS1). — Coues, Check List, 2cl ed., No. 651 (1882).—Bd., Bwr. and Ridgv., N. Am. W. Bds., I. p. 89 (1884). — Coucs, Key N. Am. Bds., p. 651 (1884). *Tantalus griscus.* Gm., Syst. Nat., I. p. 653 (1788).

Sp. Char., Male. — Terminal portion of outer primaries, greenish black, showing metallic reflections; rest of plumage, white; bare skin of head and legs, carmine in the breeding season, at other seasons much paler.

The sexes are similar.

Length 23.50; wing 10.50; tail 4; tarsus 3.40.

The white Ibis is a regular winter visitant, and probably a resident in San Domingo. The flesh is delicate, and of good flavor, and is much sought after by the natives. It is claimed that some years it is quite common, while others it is rarely seen.

No. Date. Sex. Mus. Locality. Wing. Tail. Tarsus. Hill.
3273 March «, 1883. i? C.B.C. SaJgo ,.. 4. 3. 4,So 3272 March 29,883. C. B. C. g JTM. .2. 4.5 3.5 5.5 *Plegadis faleincllus* is given by Gundlach from Porto Rico. It probably occasionally occurs in San Domingo. bluish; immature plumage entirely white or slaty gray; legs, greenish; soles of the feet, yellow. Length 29; wing 14; tail 4; tarsus 5.30; bill 3.90.

There is a great difference in the plumage of young and old birds: some adults are white, while some young birds are colored; but these are exceptions.

This species is probably resident in San Domingo. Several specimens were taken.

ARDEA CANDIDISSIMA. *Cm. Ardca nivea.* Jacq., Bertr., 18 (1784). *Ardea candidissima.* Gm., Syst. Nat., II. p. 633 (1788). — Bryant,

Proc. Bost. Soc. Nat. Hist., XI. p. 96 (1866). —Cory, Bds.

Bahama I., p. 167 (1880). *Garzctta candidissima.* Bonap., Consp., II. 119 (1855). — Bd., Bwr.

and Ridgw., N. Am. V. Bds., p. 28 (1884). *Sp. Char., Male.* — Adult, pure white; a long occipital crest of feathers, and also dorsal plumes; bill, black, yellow at the base; legs, black, yellow behind; toes, yellow; iris, yellow.

Length 22; wing 11; tarsus 3.50; bill 3.

Dr. Bryant includes this species in his list of the birds of San Domingo. It is probably a rare straggler.

ARDEA C/ERULEA. *Linn. Ardca ccerulea.* Linn., Syst. Nat., cd. 10, p. 143, No. 13 (1758);

I. p. 238, No. 17 (1766.) — Wils., Am. Orn., VII. p. 117, pi. 62 (1813).— Nutt. , Man. Orn., II. p. 58 (1834). —Aud., Bds.

Am., VI. p. 148, pi. 372 (1843). — Coucs, Key, p. 268 (1872).—

Cory, Bds. Bahama I., p. 171 (1880); Bull. Nutt. Orn. Club, VI. p. 155 (1881). *Egretta ccerulea.* Gosse, Bds. Jam., p. 337 (1847).

Florida ccerulea. Bd., Bds. N. Am., p. 671 (1858). — Gundl., Anal.

Soc. Esp. Hist. Nat., Tomo VII. p. 357 (1878).— Ridg., Nom.

N. Am. Bds., No. 493 (1881). —Bd., Bwr. and Ridgw., N. Am.

W. Bds., I. p. 43 (1884). — Coues, Key N. A. Bds., p. 661 (1884). *Ardca ceerulesccns.* Lath., Ind. Orn., II. p. 690

(1790).

Sp. Char., Male. — Slaty blue, shading into purple on the head and neck; bill, blue, becoming dark at the end; legs, black; immature plumage, pure white, generally showing a tinge of blue, usually on the primaries; legs, greenish blue; toes, yellowish.

Length about 23; wing 11; tarsus 3.60.

The present species is a winter visitant. Several specimens were taken in Haiti in February.

ARDEA VIRESCENS. Linn. *Ardea stellaris minima.* Catesby, Carolina, I. pi. 80 (1754).

Ardea virescens. Linn., Syst. Nat., ed. 10, p. 144, No. 15 (1758);

ed. 12, I. p. 238, No. 20 (1766). — Wils., Am. Orn., VII. p. 97, pi. 61 (1813). — Nutt., Man. Orn., II. p. 63 (1834). — Aud., Bds.

Am., VI. p. 105, pi. 367 (1843). — Cory, Bds. Bahama I., p. 171 (18So); Bull. Nutt. Orn. Club, VI. p. 155 (1881). *Herodias virescens.* Gosse, Bds. Jam., p. 340 (1847). *Butorides virescens.* Salle, P. Z. S., 1857, p. 236. — Bd., Bwr. and

Ridgw., N. Am. W. Bds., I. p. 50 (1884). —Coucs, Key N. Am.

Bds., p. 662 (1884). *Ardea (Butorides) virescens.* Bryant, Proc. Bost. Soc. Nat. Hist., XI. p. 97 (1866). *Ocniscus virescens.* Gundl., Anal. Soc. Esp. Hist. Nat., Tomo VII.

p. 359 (1878). *Sp. Char., Male.* — An occipital crest of dark green; neck, chestnut; throat, marked heavily with white; underparts, pale purplish or ashy, marked with white; back, greenish, showing tinge of slate color; wing coverts, green; feathers, edged with rufous white; carpus, edged with white; tail, greenish; upper mandible, black; lower mandible, mostly yellow; legs, yellowish green; upper breastfeathers lengthened into a sort of plume, covering a bare space.

Length 16; wing 6.50; tail 2.40; tarsus 1.85; bill 2.30.

A common species, probably resident, frequenting the marshes and growth bordering the lakes. Specimens were taken at Gantier and Port au Prince.

The following species probably occasionally occur in San Domingo, as they are not uncommon in Porto Rico (Gundlach) and Cuba: *Ardca herodias, Ardca oceidcntalis, Ardea egretta, Ardea leucogastra, Nyctiardea ncevia, Nyctiardea violacea, Botaurus minor,* and *Ardetta exilis.* p. 181 (1842). — Gosse, Bds. Jam., p. 355 (1847). — Salle, P. Z. S., 1857, p. 236.

"*Notherodins holostictus.* Cab., J. f. O., 1856, p. 426." *Aramus holostictus.* Scl. and Salv., Ibis, 1859, p. 227.

Sp. Char., Male. — General plumage, olivaceous brown, the feathers centrally striped with white; side flanks and crissum, grayish brown; primaries and tail, purplish chocolate, showing purple reflections; above, showing a tinge of purplish bronze; lores, chin, and throat, dull white, slightly streaked with brown; under mandible, slightly twisted near the tip. The sexes are similar.

Length 25; wing 11.50; tarsus 4.25; bill 4.10.

Two birds of this species were shot at Gantier. Specimens were also taken near Samana. The flesh is greatly esteemed by the natives.

t V FAMILY

Subfamily, PARRIN.

Genus: PARRA. Linn.

PARRA: *LINN&US, SYST. NAT., /. /.* 259, 1766.

PARRA GYMNOSTOMA. *Wagt. Parra gymnostoma.* — Wagl., Isis, 1831, p. 517. — Scl. and Salv., Nom. Av. Neotr., p. 142 (1873). — Merrill, Bull. Nutt. Orn. Club, I. p. 88 (1876). —Ridg., Nom. N. Am. Bds., No. 568 (1881). — Bd., Bwr. and Ridgw., N. Am. W. Bds., I. p. 176 (1884), — Coucs, Key N. Am. Bds., p. 669 (1884). *Parra cordifera.* — Less., Rev. Zool., 1842, p. 135. — Des Murs., Icon. Orn., pi. 42. *Parra violacea.* — Cory, Bull. Nutt. Orn. Club, VI. p. 130 (1881). *Sp. Char., Male.* — Bill and comb, pale orange; bare skin at the base of the lower mandible, pale bluish white; head, neck, arid upper breast, dark lustrous green; back and wing coverts, purple, shading into rich golden brown near the rump; rump and tail coverts, bright purple; underparts, dark purple, showing a tinge of dark rufous on the crissum; most of the primaries and secondaries, bright yellow, edged with brown; tail, rufous brown; carpal spur, pale orange; legs and feet, dull olive; iris, brown. Length 9; wing 5.50; tail 2.25; tarsus 2.25; bill 1.40. flanks, striped, and wing edged with white; crissum, whitish; bill, with frontal plate, red, sometimes edged with yellowish. Length 13; wing 6.60; tail 3.10; tarsus 2.

A single specimen taken near Le Coup, which, although somewhat brighter in coloration than specimens in my collection from Cuba and Central America, is apparently the same. It is probably a scarce resident.

This species is not uncommon about the lakes neat Gantier. Several specimens were taken.

Martinicogallinulc. Lath., Syn., III. p. 255, pi. 83 (1785). *Fulica flavirostris.* Gmel., Syst. Nat., I. p. 699 (1788). *Gallinula porphyrio.* Wils., Am. Orn., IX. p. 69, pi. 73 (1824). *Porphyrio tavona.* Vieill., Gal. Ois., II. p. 170 (1825). *Porphyrio americanus.* SV., Classif. Bds., II. p. 357 (1837). *Sp. Char., Male.* — Head, neck, and undcrparts, bluish purple, grading into black on the belly; above, olive; wing coverts, bluish; back, olive; crissum, white; frontal plate of the bill, blue; bill, red, tipped with yellow; legs, yellow.

Length 11; wing 6.50; tail 2.65; tarsus 2.30.

This beautiful bird is not uncommon near Gantier. Specimens were brought in by the natives at Le Coup.

Fulica wilsoni. Stephens, Shaw's Gen. Zobl., XII. p. 236 (1824). *Fulica atra.* Wils., Am. Orn., IX. p. 61, pi. 73, fig. 1 (1825). *Sp. Char., Male.* — Dark slate color, becoming grayish on the abdomen; head and neck, glossy blue-black; olive markings upon the back; edge of wing and ends of secondaries, white; bill, white, marked with reddish black on the upper, and a spot of the same near the end of the lower mandible; feet, dark olive.

Length 14.75; wing 7.45; tail 2.30; bill, from lower edge of frontal plate, 1.40.

This species is abundant about the lakes near Gantier, during the winter

months.
FAMILY PHOENICOPTERID:. Genus: PHCENICOPTERUS. Linn.
PHCENICOPTERUS: LINNAEUS, 1748. — *SYST. NAT, I. I.* 230, 1766.
PHCENICOPTERUS RUHER. *Linn.*
Phcenicopterus ruber. Linn., Syst. Nat. , I. loth ed. p. 139 (1758); I. I2th ed., p. 230 (1766). — Wils., Am. Orn., VIII. p. 45, pi. 66 (1814). — Nutt., Man., II. p. 70 (1834). — Aud., Bds. Am., VI. p. 169, pi. 375 (1843). —Salle (Sclater), P. Z. S., 1857, p. 236. — Bd., Cat. N. Am. Bds., No. 502 (1859). — Bryant, Proc. Bost. Soc. Nat. Hist., VII. p. 121 (1859); XI. p. 70 (1866).— Coues, Key, 1872. 278.— Gundl., Anal. Soc. Esp. Hist. Nat., Tomo VII. p. 398 (1878). — Cory, Bds. Bahama I., p. 180 (1880). —Bd., Bwr. and Ridgw., Hist. N. Am. W. Bds. , I. p. 415 (1884). *(?) Phcenicopterus glyphorhynchus.* "Gray, Ibis, 1869, pi. 14, fig. 5." *Sp. Char., Male.* — Entire plumage, scarlet; most of primaries, black; legs, lake red; terminal half of bill, black; basal half of lower mandible, orange. Young males and females are paler.
Length 52; wing 17; tail 6.50; tarsus 12. 50; bill 5.25.

One specimen was seen near Gonaives. It is known to the natives at Gantier, who claim that it is sometimes seen at the lakes.
FAMILY
Subfamily, A N A T I N Genus: DENDROCYGNA. Swain.
DENDROCYGNA: SWAIXSON, CLASS. BIRDS, II. I. 365, 1837.
DENDROCYGNA ARBOREA. *(Linn.) Anas arborca.* Linn., Syst. Nat., I. p. 207 (1766).— Gmcl., Syst. Nat. I. p. 540 (1788). —Vieill., Enc. Meth., p. 141 (1823).
Dendrocygna arborca. Eyton, Mon. Anat., p. 110 (1838). — Gosse, Bds. Jam., p. 395 (1847). — Bryant, Proc. Bost. Soc. Nat. Hist., XI. p. 70 (1866). —Scl. and Salv., P. Z. S., 1876, p. 375. — Gundl, Anal. Soc. Esp. Hist. Nat., Tomo VII. p. 400 (1878). — Cory, Bds. Bahama I., p. 183 (1880). *Anas jacquini.* "Gmel., Syst. Nat., I. p. 536 (1788). " *Sp. Char., Male.* — Head with black band on the crown, continuing in narrow stripes to the nape; forehead and over the eye, reddish brown, shading into dull white on the throat, and mottled brown and white on the sides of the head and neck; breast and t1pper parts, brown, the feathers broadly edged with tawny; rump and tail, black; underparts, brownish white, heavily spotted and banded upon the sides, the spots becoming very small and faint upon the abdomen; most of the primaries, slate color, becoming brownish at the tips; legs and bill, black.
Length 21; wing 11.25; tarsus 2.60; bill 2.

Several specimens taken in different localities. It is probably resident, but not abundant.
Sp. Char., Male. — General plumage, tawny, mottled, and streaked with brown; wing, banded with lustrous green, black, and tawny, in the order given; top of head and nape, brown, finely mottled with dark brown; rest of head and throat, white; a triangular patch on each side of the upper mandible, lake red; tail, tawny, becoming pale at the tip; legs, black.
Length 19; wing 8; tail 4.75; tarsus 1. 25; bill 1.95.
This species probably occurs in San Domingo. No specimens were taken, but I think that I saw it on two occasions. We found it abundant on the island of Inagua Bahamas.
Cyanopterus discors. Gosse, Bds. Jam., p. 401 (1847).
Anas (Querqucduld) discors. Bryant, Proc. Bost. Soc. Nat. Hist., XI. p. 97 (1866).
Sp. Char., Male. — Above, dark brown, the feathers edged and streaked with tawny; underparts, pale reddish white, thickly mottled with dull brown spots, showing a tinge of pink on the flanks and lower part of the breast; head, gray, with a purplish tinge; chin and top of the head, velvety black, the latter bordered by white, joining at the base of the crown, and continuing down the nape; a triangular white patch in front of the eye, reaching to the throat; a white patch upon either side of the tail at the base; tail-feathers, pointed, dark brown, tipped with tawny; wings showing large patches of light blue, metallic green, and white.
Female easily recognized by the absence of the white on the head.
Length 15.30; wing 7.05; tail 2.85; tarsus 1.25; bill 1.60.
Dr. Bryant records this species from San Domingo. None were met with by our party, but it is no doubt common at some seasons.

The following species probably occur in San Domingo. Gundlach records them all from Porto Rico, and they have been taken in most of the islands of the Greater Antilles: *Mareca americana, Spatula clypcata, Fuligula affinis, Fuligula collaris, Ersmatra rubida, Erismatura dominica.* FAMILY Genus: SULA. Briss.
SULA: BRISSOX, ORNITfl., 1760.
SULA CYANOPS. *Sundev. Dysporus cyanops.* Sundev., Phys. Tidskr. Lund., pt. 5 (1837).— P. Z.
S., 1871, 125. *Sula cyanops.* Sundev., Isis, 1842, p. 858. — Salv., Trans. Zool. Soc., IX. 496 (1875).—Bd., Bwr. and Ridgw., Hist. N. Am.
W. Bds., II. p. 176 (1884). *Sula dactylatra.* Bryant, Proc. Bost. Soc. Nat. Hist. , VII. p. 125 (1859); XI. p. 97 (1866). — Cory, Bds. Bahama I., p. 194 (1880).
Sp. Char., Afale. — Sexes similar; larger than 6". *leucogastra;* "secondaries and tertiaries, rich brown, the primaries of the same color, but darker; some of the coverts of the primaries, brownish; tail, with the feathers below, brown; above, hoary, the two middle feathers the most so, and the base of all, white or whitish; all the rest of the plumage, snowy white; bill, horn color, with the serrations of the upper mandible very distinctly marked; iris, pale yellow; eyes and throat, black; tarsi and feet, yellowish green"; bare skin of face and gular sac, bluish. coverts and shafts of tail-feathers, black; tail extended into two very long feathers, which are reddened; tarsus, bluish; iris, black; webs and toes, black.
Wing 16.35; ta'l 7-50; tarsus 1.85; bill 4.

This species is given by Dr. Bryant in his list, and I have included it on his au-

SULA LEUCOGASTRA. *(Bodd.) Pelecanus leucogaster.* Bodd., Tabl. P. E., p. 57 (1783). *Dysporus Icucogaster.* Sundev., P. Z. S., 1871-, 125. *Sula leHcogaslra.* Salv., Trans. Zool. Soc., IX. p. 496 (1875). — Bd., Bwr. and Ridgw., Hist. N. Am. W. Bds., II. p. 178 (1884). *Sula fusca.* And., Bds. N. Am., VII. p. 57 (1844) (not *P. fuscus,* Z.).—Bryant, Proc. Bost. Soc. Nat. Hist., XI. p. 97 (1866). *Sula fiber.* Lawr., in Baird's Bds. N. A., 872 (1858) (not *P. fiber, L.).* — Bryant, Proc. Bost. Soc. N. Hist., VII. p. 123 (1859).— Coues, Key N. Am. Bds., p. 298 (1872). — Scl. and Salv. , Nom. Avium Neot., p. 124 (1873). — Cory, Bds. Bahama I., p. 191 (1880). *Sp. Char., Male.* — Head, throat, upper part of breast, and entire upper plumage, dark olive brown; under parts, white; gular sac, pale yellow; upper mandible, greenish; feet, pale yellowish green; iris, yellowish.

Length 27; wing 15.50; tail 8; tarsus 1. 60; bill 4.

Probably not uncommon in summer, although none were seen by our party. Dr. Bryant records it in his list.

FAMILY PELECANID:. Genus: PELECANUS. Linn.

PELECANUS: LINKSEUS, SYST. NAT., i — *SYST. XAT., I. /.* 132, 1758.

PELECANUS FUSCUS. *(Linn.) Pelecaln1s fuscus.* Linn., Syst. Nat., I. p. 215 (1766).— Vieill., Gal. Ois., t. 276. — Nutt., Man., II. p. 476 (1834).— Aud. , Bds. Am., VII. p. 32, pis. 423, 424 (1844). — Gosse, Bds. Jam., p. 409 (1847).— Bryant, Proc. Best. Sue. Nat. Hist., VII. p. 122 (1859).— Lavr., in Baird's Bds. N. Am., p. 870 (1858).— Cory, Bds. Bahama I., p. 196 (1880). — Coues, Check List, 2d ed., No. 749 (1882).— Bd., Bvr. and Ridgw., Hist. N. Am. W. Bds., II. p. 139 (1884). *Leptopclicanus fuscus.* Reich., Syst. Av., VII. (1852). *Onoerotalus fuscus.* Bp., Consp., II. p. 163, 1854. *Sp. Char., Male.* — Sac, dark purple; above, slate color, and dark brown variegated; neck of the adult, reddish brown; head, mostly white; bill, darker, marked with red; feet, purplish black; iris, yellowish.

Females generally have the neck yellowish white.

Length 53; wing 18; tail 7.40; tarsus 2.50; bill 10.

The present species is common to some portions of the coast. Several were seen near Port an Prince in February. We also saw it near St. Mark.

V *Sp. Char., Male.* — Entire plumage, brownish black, showing a greenish reflection on the head, and purplish upon the back; tail forked, and composed of twelve feathers; gular sac, pale orange; iris, brown.

Sp. Char., Female.— Differs from the male by having a white patch on the breast, passing along the sides of the neck, and around near the middle.

Length 43; wing 25; tail 19; tarsus 1; bill 6.

This species is common, and probably resident. A number of specimens were shot by our party, but as a rule they were very shy and difficult to obtain.

Length, including tail-feathers, 31. 50; wing u; tail 21; tarsus 90; bill 2.

This graceful bird cannot be common in San Domingo, as I did not meet with it. Dr. Bryant gives it in his list, and I include it on his authority.

Sp. Char., Male.— Bill, lake red; hood, grayish black; nape, white, forming a sort of collar; upper parts, pearl gray; beneath, white; outer primaries, dark brown; tail, white; feet, black, with red on the webs; iris, dark brown.

Length 15.50; wing 12.50; tail 5; tarsus 1.90; bill 1.40.

The Laughing Gull visits San Domingo during the summer months, and probably breeds, although we were unable to find its eggs, and comparatively few birds were seen.

Sterna rcgia. Gamb., Proc. Acad. Nat. Sci. Phila., 1848, p. 228.— Bryant, Proc. Bost. Soc. Nat. Hist., VII. p. 134 (1859); XI. p. 98 (1866). — Lawr., in Baird's Bds. N. Am., p. 859 (1858).— Coues, Check List, No. 562 (1873). — Cory, Bds. Bahama I., p. 210 (1880). —Ridw., Nom. N. Am. Bds., No. 681 (1881). *Thalasscus regius.* Gamb., Journ. Phila. Acad., I. 2d ser., p. 228 (1849). — Coues, Pr. Phila. Acad., 1862, p. 539.— Gundl., Anal. Soc. Esp. Hist. Nat., Tomo VII. p. 410 (1878).

Thalasseus cayanus. Gosse, Bds. Jam., p. 431 (1847). *Sp. Char., Afale.*--- Bill, orange, reddish at the base; above, pearl gray; primaries, showing much white on the inner webs; crown, black, the feathers extending in a sort of crest to the back; below, white; tail, white and forked.

Length 19; wing 14.50; tail 7.50; tarsus 1.25; bill 2.25.

I include this species on the authority of Dr. Bryant, as we did not find it. It undoubtedly occurs, but is probably not abundant.

1876, p. 661. --- Gundl., Anal. Soc. Esp. Hist. Nat., Tomo VII. p. 412 (1878).— Ridgw., Nom. N. Am. Bds., II. No. 690 (1881).—Bd., Bwr. and Ridgw., Hist. N. Am. W. Bds., II. p. 309 (1884). *Sterna snperciliaris, b. antillarum.* Coues, Check List, 2d cd.

No. 801 (1882). *Sterna frenata.* Gamb. , Proc. Acad. Nat. Sci. Phila., 1848, p. 128.

— Lawr., in Baird's Bds. N. Am., p. 864 (1858).— Baird, Cat.

N. Am. Bds., No. 694 (1859). *Sterna superciliaris.* Gundl. and Cab., J. f. O., V. p. 232 (1857).—

Coues, Check List, No. 570 (1873). — Cory, Bds. Bahama I., p. 213(1880). *Sp. Char., Male.* --- Bill, yellow, tipped with black; cap, black forehead, white; above, pearly gray; underparts, white; outer primaries, dark brown on the outer webs and inner half of inner webs; tail, white, forked; coverts, pearl gray; legs, pale yellow; iris, brown.

Length 8.75; wing 6.50; tail 2.20; tarsus.55; bill 1.

The species is common in summer, and probably breeds.

STERNA FULIGINOSA. *Cm. Sterna fuliginosa.* Gmel., Syst. Nat., I. p. 605 (1788). — Wils., Am. Orn., VIII. p. 145, pi. 72, fig. 7 (1814). — Nutt., Man., II. p. 284 (1834).-— Aud., Bds. Am., VII. p. 90, pi. 432 (844).---- Lawr., in Baird's Bds. N. Am., p. 861 (1858).— Baird, Cat. N. Am. Bds., No. 688 (1889).— Bryant, Proc. Bost. Soc. Nat. Hist., VII. p. 134 (1859); XI. p. 98 (1866). —Saunders, P. Z. S., 1876, p. 666. — Cory, Bds. Bahama I., p. 214 (1880). Coues, Check List, 2d ed., No. 804

(1882). — Bd., Bwr. and Ridgw., Hist. N. Am. W. Bds., II. p. 312 (1884). *Strna (Haliplana fuliginosa.* Coues, Key, p. 322 (1872). *Sterna serrata.* Forst., Descr. An. ed. Licht., 1844, p. 276. *Sterna guttata.* Forst., Descr. An. ed. Licht., 1844, p. 211. *Anous r Herminieri.*— Less., Descr. Man. et. Ois., p. 255 (1847). *Sterna luctuosa.* Phil, and Laudb., Wiegm. Archiv., 1866, p. 126. *Sterna fuliginosa var. erissalis.* "Baird," Lawr., Proc. Bost. Soc. Nat. Hist., 1871, p. 285. *Hydrochelidon fuliginosa.* Gosse, Bds. Jam., p. 433 (1847). *Haliplana fuliginosa.* Gundl., Anal. Soc. Esp. Hist. Nat., Tomo VII. p. 414 (1878). *Sp. Char., Male.* — Bill, black; crown and entire upper plumage, black; forehead, white; extending into a pair of horns not reaching above the eye; underparts, white; outer tail-feathers, white, showing very dark brown for about two inches on the inner webs near the tip; legs, black; iris, brown.

Length 16.50; wing 11.50; tail 7; tarsus. 90; bill 1.60.

This species is found on the uninhabited reefs and small islands during the summer months, and probably breeds.

Sterna anostlusta probably occurs in San Domingo, as it is common, and breeds in the Bahamas; but we did not find it, and it has yet to be recorded. *Anous stolidus var. frater.* Coues, Bds. N. W., p. 712 (1874).

Megalopterus stolidus. Gossc, Bds. Jam., p. 434 (1847).

Sterna (Anous) stolida. Bryant, Proc. Bost. Soc. Nat. Hist., XI. p. 97 (1866).

Sp. Char., Male.— Bill, black; forehead, white, shading into gray at the base of the skull; lower eyelid, white; front of the eye and narrow superciliary line, blackish; entire plumage, rich olive brown; primaries, dark brown, the first having the inner web pale brown; legs, black; iris, dark brown.

Length 15; wing 10; tail 5.75; tarsus.80; bill 1.70.

This species is common in summer, and breeds in some localities on the coast.

The following species are recorded from some of the Greater Antilles, and probably occur in San Domingo: *Sterna cantiaca. Sterna dougalli,* and *Hydrochelidon lariformis.* FAMILY PROCELLARID:.

Subfamily, PROCELL A R I N/E.

Genus: PUFFINUS. Briss. *PUFFIXUS: BRISSO.V, ORNITH., VI. p. y,* 1760.

PUFFINUS OBSCURUS. *(Cm.)*

Procellaria obscura. Gmcl., Syst. Nat., I. p. 559 (1788).— Bryant, Proc. Bost. Soc. Nat. Hist., XI. p. 98 (1866).

Puffinus obscurns. Bp., Syn., p. 371 (1828). — Nutt., Man., II. P-337 (1834). —Aud., Bds. Am., VII. p.. 216, pi. 458 (1844).— Lawr., in Baird's Bds. N. Am., p. 835 (1858). — Bryant, Proc. Bost. Soc. Nat. Hist., VII. p. 132 (1859). —Cory, Bds. Bahama I., p. 219 (1880). —Coues, Check List, 20! cd., No. 835 (1882).

Fujjinus auduboni. Finsch, P. Z. S., 1872, p. 111. — Ridgw., Nom. N. Am. Bds., No. 712 (1881).— Bd., Bwr. and Ridgw., Hist. N. Am. W. Bds., II. p. 386 (1884). *Sp. Chaf., Jlfale.* — Above, glossy brown, shading into grayish upon the sides of the breast; below, white; crissum, brown and white; tail, brown, the feathers faintly tipped with ashy; bill, lead color.

Length 12.50; wing 8; tail 4.25; tarsus 1.60; bill 1.30.

Dr. Bryant records this species from San Domingo. None were met with by our party, although a number were seen while at sea about twenty miles north of Tortuga I.

Sp. Char., llale. — Above, dark brown, with slight greenish reflections; sides of the head and throat, ashy gray, continuous in a broad band around the neck; underparts, silky white, mottled with dusky; outer primaries, showing chocolate brown, the others and secondaries, white.

Length 9.35; wing 3.60; tarsus 1.24; bill.85.

This pretty little species is probably not uncommon, although we did not meet with it. I have included it on Dr. Bryant's *J* authority, as given in his list.